Thank you for purchasing Winning Online!

Congratulations! You have taken the first-step toward improving your online visibility; and over time, you will crush your competition, if you stick with the framework and key principles shared with you in these pages. To give you a jump-start, I decided to also share an easy-to-read resource that will show you:

The 5 things your website <u>must have</u> to attract new customers.

It's my gift to you!

As an added bonus, and thank you for investing in yourself by purchasing 'Winning Online', you will also receive 2 months to try Your Own Review Platform for free ($100 Value): it's the same platform Daniel used in the case-story you are about to read.

Simply go to: www.winningonlinebook.com *and claim your <u>two free</u> gifts now!*

WINNING ONLINE

*Increase Your
Visibility and Crush
Your Competition!*

JOEL MANDELBAUM

Table of Content

Chapter 1 1
The Early Years

Chapter 2 13
Chasing Two Rabbits

Chapter 3 38
One Step Forward, Two Steps Back

Chapter 4 49
The Lake: Part 1 (Website Communication)

Chapter 5 69
The Lake: Part 2 ("Search-Engine Marketing")

Chapter 6 88
The Lake: Part 3 ("Review Marketing")

Chapter 7 103
The Commitment ("Facebook Marketing")

Chapter 8 113
"Putting It All Together"

Chapter 9 127
Scaling-Up!

Chapter 10 145
Taking-Flight! (2014 through 2018)

Chapter 11 164
How Did We Get Here, Me!

10 Steps to Winning Online! 170

FOREWORD

When the idea of writing a book like 'Winning Online' was presented almost a year ago, my first thought was… absolutely! For the last few years, I have wanted to share what I've learned with a wider audience than the consulting clients I am grateful to work with every day. While it's satisfying to see their business progress and the results accelerate, I think anyone in my position, would want to get this knowledge into the hands of a greater number of business leaders, like you.

Sure, there was a moment of doubt: should I release what I've learned and developed over the years – my secrets and industry insider insights – to the general public, including my competition? But at the same time, I realized that the landscape of online marketing is constantly evolving into fresh conditions, where new tools and innovative technologies are introduced at breakneck speed almost daily. What I'm sharing with you is my perspective and understanding of how the pieces all fit together, and how to use this knowledge for the benefit of you and your company.

My goal is that by the time you finish reading this book, you will have the ability to crush your competition online – rather than being left behind by technology and innovation, as I once was. See, there was a time in my life when I did not fully appreciate or understand the changing conditions the internet brought to a business.

I was left behind, and it cost me dearly.

Having started a business at 19 with little more than grit and a few dollars in my pocket, I learned the hard way: how to sell, how to grow and manage a company, and how to lead a team of dedicated people, while developing an understanding and appreciation of the conditions that customers experience. In our case, clients relied on us to fulfill a crucial role in their supply chain. In our heyday, we were an award-winning company, growing leaps and bounds every year, in Canada and the U.S. Those were exciting times!

But in the latter years, we stayed the course with what brought us to that point of success; what we knew *had* worked in the past. And we thought it would continue to carry us forward, while technology and market preferences changed how users sought out service providers like us. Looking back now, I'd have to describe our online presence as the barest of minimums, even by standards in those days...

I used to think that failure was unacceptable; that it was a result of weakness, not working hard enough, or simply giving up. But I realized, after going through the experience, that it was none of the above. It was a valuable gift, wrapped-up as a learning experience. Selling the business allowed what we had built over the years to continue on: most of our staff kept their jobs, our loyal clients to this day receive the service they need and deserve; and for me, it marked the single greatest learning period of my life. That gift has since rewarded me many times over and continues to do so. I am so grateful for that "failure", I would not be where I am today without it.

My Appreciation:

Writing this book has been an adventure, to say the least. And it would not have been possible without three groups of very special people in my life. First of course are my family, friends, and especially my wife Alana. As you might know yourself, it's not easy being married to an entrepreneur. She has stuck with me during the most challenging of times: phases of life and business that only the strongest of women can persevere through, all the while supporting and encouraging her partner… Thank you Alana, I love you!

Likewise, the 'Winning Online' framework is a reality because of the many mentors, advisors, clients, and peers that I have had the privilege of working with and learning from over the years.

Equally importantly, these words would not have been written without the respect and admiration I have for you the reader. Whether you are an early-stage entrepreneur, established business owner, or developing online-marketer, I recognize what it takes to learn and adapt in these most dynamic of business eras; where keeping up with changing marketing technology and business conditions is almost a full-time job in itself. I'm fortunate that my role allows me to stay current with the leading edge of online marketing: where useful, effective, and profitable online activities are accessible to every business leader today. At the same time, it is disappointing to learn about some of the questionable online services that continue to crop up – those that, IMHO, could be characterized as snake oil. Like all industries, there are people in marketing that will make a buck by exploiting the consumers' limited subject matter knowledge. **This is one of the three reasons I decided to write this book for you:**

1. To show you *which* online marketing methods and tools produce results
2. To help you develop a fundamental understanding of effective online marketing strategies
3. To give you a step-by-step method for putting this knowledge into action

The industry secrets and insights I am sharing with you are intended to give you 100X to 1000X the value of the cost of this book and the time you spend absorbing the information. To help you capitalize on the content, I took a non-traditional approach to the text and how it's conveyed.

How to get the most out of this book:

My initial idea was to write a simple 'how to' guide to walk you through a logical sequence of steps to help understand and implement the concepts. But what I realized while outlining the content, is that we all absorb information differently, and at varying rates.

The story you are about to read, is a fictional account of one business owner's journey – drawn from real-life experiences, within a diversity of industries: serving clients with unique business conditions and challenges. It is my goal, that through reading Danny's story – his learning of online marketing strategies from Josh, and applying that learning – you will understand how to adapt your business for success, in today's constantly changing online and offline environment.

At the end of each chapter, please take the time to review the summary and consider the key concepts portrayed within the story; and most importantly, explore how they relate to your primary product or service, your industry, and the current 'state' of your business.

Do your best to be objectively honest with yourself throughout this process… the future of your business depends on it!

I hope you enjoy the read, and that the information enables you to achieve greater success online.

Sincerely,

Joel Mandelbaum

CHAPTER 1
The Early Years

It was a liberating and somewhat terrifying day, to say the least.

The matching mahogany desk and credenza set were all but completely covered with cardboard banker-boxes, file folders, family photos, and stacks of leather-bound legal texts – some I had collected personally; many were inherited from my father: himself a fine attorney in his day.

Methodically packing the last of my personal belongings into the box labelled #11 of 11 – I couldn't help but re-play in my mind some of the contradictory voices of friends and family reactions to my decision to leave the firm and go-it alone.

For almost fourteen years, the team at Samson, Thompson & Partners LLP were my co-workers, my friends – and gratefully, they were my teachers, and mentors.

As a young attorney fresh out of law school, Peter Samson was my mentor from the first year forward; taking me under his wing, opening my eyes to what was possible with determination and good old-fashioned hard work. He was a mountain of a man in stature – with a slow, deep-baritone

Kentucky drawl – and an easy-going temperament to match. Unexpected in a founder and head of a leading local law firm; Pete's affable character was his secret weapon: often underestimated by his opponents in the courtroom, or at the boardroom-table during high-stakes negotiations.

To say I learned a lot from 'big Pete' (as he was known to his closest friends) would be a tremendous understatement. I owe a great deal of my success today, to his stewardship and guidance over those early years. A collector of quotes, his borrowed parting words of advice that day, still echo in my mind when things don't go my way in the courtroom, in business, or in life: "Daniel", he said, "All life is an experiment. The more experiments you make the better"[1]… and "try not to become a man of success, rather become a man of value"[2].

We never spoke in detail about my reasons for leaving. But in those last few years, looking back now, I think Pete and the rest of the partners recognized that I might have that entrepreneurial 'fire in the belly'. And the idea of setting up my own company only intensified following our merger with Steadman LLP: a multi-regional firm that had the reach and resources to propel Samson et al to the next level – into a substantial, truly full-service law firm, capable of competing with the region's top legal practises.

The transition was as smooth as a merger *can* be. What brought the notion of my exit to the forefront was that I couldn't see myself being happy at the next level – as a full partner.

A long Sunday-afternoon talk with my wife Melissa was all it took to make the decision. We set out to provision and plan for the first few years – it would be a stretch, and Melissa's accounting training and natural knack for numbers would be the backbone of what we thought was a well-prepared transition to self employment.

While it was almost ten years ago, I will never forget the day we opened the doors of 'The Davidson Firm' for the very first time: Monday, December 15, 2008. The region had just been hit with a 3-day lake-effect storm that blanketed the quiet rural town of Orchard Park, New York with nearly four feet of thick, heavy snow; drifting in some areas reached as high as 7 feet. I lucked-out – picking up the last snow blower from Arthur's Hardware store, and set out to clear the pathway leading up to our new storefront office on West Quaker street. That day was frustrating. A face-numbing nor'easter blew fast and furious; replacing about twenty-five percent of my snow-clearing effort with a few inches of fresh white stuff, every five minutes or so.

And within a week, a second storm engulfed the region over a 2-day period; dropping another three feet on an already devasted community; ill prepared for an early-season double-dumping. Tragically, during that stretch, three people passed from heart attack; suffered as a result of over-exertion while clearing drive and walk-ways of family homes and local businesses, using snow shovels.

But the community rallied together in support of one another, like small towns tend to do in troubling times. Neighbours broke bread with neighbours who had lost power; teens and young adults shuttled food on foot to the elderly, and the local snowmobile club made their rounds to make sure everyone was safe and accounted for.

I can't complain about spending several days moving mountains of snow under a heavy coat and three layers of clothing, nonetheless – at the time – I could not help but wonder, if those overly challenging conditions in the early days of The Davidson Firm, were an omen of what was to follow…

Turns out, it was.

The first two years were as expected. Billings were bare-able based on our projections, and we were just shy of break-even in year 2; not bad for an environmental law practise with one relatively large-billing, 'anchor' client, less than a handful of smaller ones on retainer, and a new service we were planning to expand into markets beyond the Western New York region. Thankfully, Melissa kept our business and household expenses in-check: we didn't discretionary-spend over a-hundred-dollars without consulting the Quickbooks budget she kept up to date, near daily.

About a quarter of the way through year 3, Melissa and I began to stress about the state of our finances and how we should go about growing our base of business – that had to hit a monthly billables target of $9,300, to keep the company and household from going further into debt. Melissa's part-time business managing 'the books' for a handful of small, local companies was a godsend; especially when cash flow would occasionally slow to a trickle. I had to find the answers to growing our sales; and fast. The financial pressure was beginning to take its toll on our relationship.

While an attorney at Samson, Thompson & Partners, prospects were mostly attracted to the firm using radio, print, and an annual, spring T.V. advertising campaign, along with heavy networking efforts by the partners. Associates like me, were encouraged to build a network and bring new business to the firm; a pre-requisite for partnership some day. Associates that produced results, were recognized and rewarded when annual bonus time came around in early February. For Melissa and I, those bonuses were used for vacations, reno's on the house, and during the early, 'leaner' years, we applied the majority of my bonus to principal payments on our mortgage.

I had worked hard to develop a solid network, and sacrificed many evenings with Melissa and social occasions with friends and family. Now that I was on my own, it was even more important that I deepen and expand relationships with centers of influence in the surrounding towns, and the region's major cities of Buffalo, Rochester, and Syracuse, New York.

For the effort, I brought in two new, small corporate clients, and a third came from a referral. But my specialization in environmental law was mostly beyond the scope of potential clients that my existing network would typically interact with. The stark reality was, that I would need to either find, court, and close another anchor client, or figure out how to bring in a consistent stream of smaller billable clients, from our new legal service: processing 'claims'. Hundreds of thousands of people across the country were qualified to make a claim under various government compensation programs, for workers who became ill as a result of their job – and a great deal of them needed help navigating through the system. The key would be figuring out how to find those people – or more likely, help them to find me.

I recognized that to reach those prospects, I would need to become a better marketer. Print advertising was already generating qualified leads for us, and it was profitable. I thought at the time: how hard could it be to translate those results to online marketing? I liked the idea of reaching thousands of prospects with the click of a mouse.

And I liked the idea of representing *claimants*; of being on the other side of the argument, for a change. At Samson, we always represented the defendants in environmental cases: large corporations with deep pockets, and a combination in-house and hired legal team – that often approached the size and expertise level of a typical Major League Baseball squad. I wouldn't characterize my skills in those days, alongside the 'first-string' litigators I worked with, but I did learn from many of the 'star' attorneys – that developing a compelling case is best-approached by understanding the opposition's perspective, as clearly as our own. I suppose that is what partly drew me to help people collect the compensation they were due. They had been irreparably harmed while simply doing their job, and that I might make a substantial living in support of *their* cause; well, that was something that would be difficult to pass up.

Melissa wasn't as convinced as I was – that the Davidson Firm should specialize in a fairly narrow sub-set of environmental law. And after supper one Sunday evening in February, we talked out our options: the pros and cons; at the dinner table, over a bottle of Bordeaux.

We had agreed from the outset, that two brains are better than one when it comes down to pivotable business decisions – like this one. I have always trusted and respected the objectivity in her opinions. As the daughter of a civil-engineer father, and journalist mother, it's not surprising how her balanced perspective developed from an early age.

But in the discussion that night, I think fear had more of an influence on her position than what she might have wanted to admit at the time. Our regular – point, counter-point – method of working through differences, was abandoned unintentionally after only about 20 minutes into it. On the business development side, she argued that one of my strengths was relationship building, and reasoned that by focussing on more targeted networking environments – local and across the state – it was just a matter of time before I would land another anchor client; or at the very least, uncover a more generalized corporate litigation client, given my past track record in the courtroom.

In a way, she was right.

But her trump card, was drawing attention to my lack of experience in marketing. A law practise, centered around representing a significant volume of injured parties, was just as much about marketing the firm and its service, as it was the actual skills and work required to assess, fight, and win cases.

Eventually, we agreed that the firm's success would be dependent on our ability to market its services, whether they were litigation-based or any other.

What I was attempting to help Melissa see, was that you can fish where the big fish swim, but those fishing holes are already crowded with an abundance of baited poles; all competing to lure, hook, and land the same 'prize-winning' fish. My vision, was to uncover a niche that provided the opportunity to eventually 'scale-up' marketing, customer service, and the operations functions – as we learned and developed a sound system for each.

As I continued to explain – slowly, Melissa began to take a softer line. And what she didn't yet know, was that a few years prior, I came across an attorney on the west coast, that was earning a decent living from those types of cases alone; just himself and one part-time administrator. I contended that with an efficient admin system to process the work, we could hire, train, and build a near-limitless team of bright, energetic staff that would grow as the volume of incoming claims increased, year over year. The best part was that our employees would not need to be experienced, nor educated, attorneys, or even paralegals; opening up our hiring flexibility, and widening the field of potential, high-quality candidates.

She was right about our online marketing efforts early-on: we would need to contract out for a period of time, while I learned that aspect of the business. Melissa conceded that I was a quick learner, but it was here, that we arrived at her sticking point: could we afford to hire a company to help us market the business to a larger audience?

To date, the simply-worded classified ads in the Buffalo News were reaching our mostly 'Baby-Boomer' target market; they produced results, and they were profitable. Local potential claimants were calling the office to enquire about our service.

We were processing claims, getting them approved, being paid and making money with a straight-forward process. For me, that was all the proof I needed. And besides, I pointed out: travelling across the state to generate litigation client leads, would cost about the same as outsourced marketing.

After almost two and a half hours of discussion, and more than a few heated words – we emptied the last of the '06 Cabernet into each of our glasses, and reached a compromise. I would scale back the number of conferences and events, and continue to network. We would source an online marketing company to update our website and work with us to more heavily promote our new service. Melissa would track the revenue from each of the two client groups, and we would 'take it a month at a time', until there was a clear winner: *'Daniel Davidson litigator'* or *'Daniel Davidson claims-processing attorney'*.

Back then, that decision appeared conservative, measured, and logical to the both of us; even if it was made under the influence of a fine red wine, and more emotion than either of us were proud of at the time.

What neither of us knew though, was that the ensuing four years, would turn-out to be a tumultuous roller-coaster ride, that neither of us were prepared for: a struggle to hold onto our marriage, to stave off insolvency, and make it back from the brink of nearly losing everything – including my life.

The fact is, I would not be writing these words today, if it were not for a very special person being introduced into my life – at a time when I had just about given up all hope. In private, I refer to him as my guru, of sorts. In truth, he is a 'master' online-marketer, well-rounded business expert, and remarkably generous human being. His sage advice and counsel have been a privilege and a gift, that I am compelled to share with anyone who will listen.

Today, I have a tremendously thriving business and fulfilling life, because of the time he so generously donated to me, from early Summer till late December 2012.

Since then, we have grown to fifty-seven full-time employees (including Melissa and I), and we project that number to be well-beyond 80, within a year or so. Our dynamic team comes to work everyday with a smile on their face, and a commitment to make a difference in the lives of our clients, their co-workers, and of course, for the prosperity of the firm.

Times like these, I have to ask myself: "how did we get here"?

Especially now, as I prepare to deliver a speech next month at the 2018 Business Excellence Awards. I can't help but recall those first two weeks – back at the *first* Orchard Park office – snow hammering down, frigid temperatures – and the unrelenting, bitter cross-wind numbing my exposed cheeks, as the snow-blower carved out a path, as best it could.

But what I remember most, is the occasional uncertain thoughts I had about the future of The Davidson Firm. Would it still be around five, ten, or fifteen years later? Would I learn… could I learn – the things that I didn't know I didn't know – back then, and over the years?

While at times it took the expertise of a guru – these last 10 years have taught me that whether conditions are dire or moderately favourable – on the upswing of success, or the downfall of past mistakes – it takes a modest person to earnestly hear what can be learned: with an open mind, and an open heart.

Perhaps, this is the story *you* are intended to hear, now…

CHAPTER 2
Chasing Two Rabbits

Looking downward from 5100 feet – flying just over 140 knots – the tree-top canopy of mostly Maples, Willows, and Tamaracks looked like a vast, dense field of mixed-season broccoli. The contrasting colors were mesmerizing from up there: the deepest of greens; others, closer to moss; and occasionally a dull olive. All interrupted in spots, by random clusters of vibrant Red Maples.

As I shifted my gaze forward, toward the horizon – from the passenger seat of Big Pete's Cessna 206 Amphibian – I was grateful that Melissa had talked me into accepting Pete and Robyn's invitation, to join them for the Memorial Day long-weekend, at their lake-front cottage in the Muskoka region of Ontario, Canada.

Lost in the view through the front windscreen – suddenly, Pete's deep-drawl faintly buzzed in my headset; the words barely audible over the near-deafening, engine's roar.

I shook my head from side to side a few times, and raised an open hand to my ear – so that he would repeat himself.

"There's Rosseau, Danny – d'ya see it!?" he yelled through the intercom, so I could make out the message. "About fifteen miles northwest of us", he added; while pointing toward a large body of water, visible ahead and to the left of the whirling, double-blade prop. Seeing the outline of the shore, it most- closely resembled a large oval from the air; and a long, boot-shaped island – positioned close to dead-center – intersected just about the entire lake, from north to south.

With a nod, a smile, and a short "ah, yes!" I leaned forward to get a better look at our destination for the weekend. From what I'd read, Lake Rosseau and its surrounding region, had evolved over the decades, from a modest cottage-retreat for the upper-middle class, into what many now refer to as 'The Hamptons of the North'.

From our current altitude and distance, I could make out a number of man-made structures along the shoreline: some sat centered, within their relatively large, tree-less clearing – set back about fifty or so feet from the shore – while others were nestled lakeside; discreetly, within the trees.

Not ten minutes later, we had descended to about 1800 feet. But not before a number of stomach-turning, uneasy moments of turbulence – dipping and climbing in alteration like an amusement park roller-coaster ride. In a small aircraft, you feel and hear everything; and admittedy I was a little nervous. Not so much about the gusts at 1800 feet, as the wind and water conditions on the lake, for landing. Pete had warned us before take-off at Toronto's Billy Bishop Airport – that the

Muskoka region's wind and wake levels were unseasonably high, and that we should be prepared for a rough, bumpy ride on approach, and when the pontoons hit the water. (Being my first time in a small, private plane, I thought it would be helpful to be prepared for what I was in for, and watched a few archived online videos a couple weeks prior. Not a good idea. Of the most-serious small aircraft accidents – all but one, were a pontoon-landing, on water!). Needless to say, my anxiety level was a little more elevated than would otherwise be considered normal at that point.

We began to bank left a few miles beyond the north-east shoreline of the lake, in preparation for a north to south straight approach and landing, to the west of Rosseau's boot-shaped, Tobin Island. I took a few long, slow, deep breaths, and reminded myself that I was not in control of the plane, the conditions, or much of anything.

Recalling that we were about to spend three relaxing days in the company of two amazing people – at one of the most beautiful and tranquil places on earth – a satisfied smile eased its way back onto my face; and a quiet calm, slowly returned to the body.

With the challenges of business and finances occupying so many of my waking hours these past 17 months, I thought to myself: if ever there was a time that I needed a complete change of scenery and pace for a few days, it was now…

But first, we would need to successfully land the plane.

...

January 2011, I was committed to the plan: to split my new-business development time, effort, and resources between networking for litigation prospects, and promoting the newly-established claims processing service, to a wider audience. To help manage the workflow, we contracted a part-time paralegal for three days a week: Cassy spent half of her days doing case-law research for litigation: 'motions' and 'briefs'; and the remainder, administering about 60% of the compensation claims that came in. And to support the work required for Grayson Inc. – our largest litigation client, I informally partnered with a relatively-local attorney based out of Buffalo, New York – an easy twenty-minute drive between our offices.

When I was not travelling, out networking, or processing the remaining 40% of claims myself, many evenings were dedicated to learning the basics of online marketing techniques – those that most companies were using, back then. The plan was to hire a local firm soon.

Three months into that routine, and it was already beginning to take its toll on both of us; though at the time, I would have described my work/life imbalance, as a natural symptom of being a relatively new, self-employed owner of a small firm. With Cassy on-board, our profit was about the same, even though our billings were up 20% for the first quarter. Still, the revenue jump was enough encouragement to continue burning the candle at both ends – fully expecting, that an eventually more- profitable company would afford us some personal and family time, at some point. Mistake #1.

'XTS Design' had been on-board as our new web-marketing vendor, for about four weeks. A small company of three managing partners: their combination of experience, in-house skills, and price-point, we found to be the most value-based option, within our budget at the time.

Initially, I did not realize how much up-front work was required of *us*, to rebuild the firm's website. And there was a sense of urgency to updating it as quickly as possible – the current version was adequate, at best, for litigation prospects to view; but being our initial website, it made no mention of our claims-processing service. Melissa contributed as best she could in-between her bookkeeping, accounting and admin work for the firm; plus, *her* clients: now seven, and growing.

Together, we mapped out the information we thought was most vital for prospects to learn about the firm's services; reviewed many of our competitor's websites, and read-up on as much as we could absorb about marketing communication strategy. XTS provided us a template of necessary content areas to be covered, and a list of questions for us to include and answer, to satisfy target visitors to davidsonfirm.com. The biggest challenge was: how to 'position' the firm, given that it was offering services to two very different target groups, with clearly contrasting objectives: defendants and claimants. I recognized that the 'home' page would provide a first impression of The Davidson Firm; and visitors would need to quickly relate to the problems we solved, if we were to grab their attention, and keep them on the website long enough to learn about why our service was best for them. It was important to relate, with the first words the viewer would read. And for me, those target viewers were claimants.

Again, Melissa and I had a significant difference of opinion.

There really was no 'right' answer: to which prospect group's service should take precedence. Both were equally viable, as businesses on their own. It was still early days for our claims processing service, and although its revenue level was still far behind that of 'litigation', it was growing. And for me, it was uplifting to have business come to us, from inbound promotion; rather than by seeking, qualifying, following up, and following up again, with corporate prospects. I have never had an aversion to hard work. It just made far more sense not to stake our future on a business whose growth was, more or less, limited by the scarcest of all resources: my time.

On the other hand, I could not disagree with Melissa. Corporate clients paid the bills.

The solution we eventually agreed, was to present my experience and track record as the introductory focal-point for the firm's two service categories. In retrospect, I would describe the top thirty-five percent of the 'home' page – what visitors saw first – as 'generic-corporate' content; as was common in those days for large, notable, full-service legal practises.

All in all, I think we did a good job of representing the firm as professional, proven, and skilled. For their part, XTS did a fine job on the website's design, layout, and ease of navigation. They spent a lot of time in the courting stage, advising us how important proper 'search engine optimization' (SEO) was to prospects finding our 'site organically online. At the time, we were optimistic that the revised version of davidsonfirm.com, would generate more calls into the office, in the months to follow.

And it did.

By early July, the combination of organic search, paid online advertising, website blog, and print advertising gave our claims processing revenue a lift of almost 23%; quarter over quarter. By comparison, those revenues were still substantially lower than what corporate clients generated; nonetheless, we were on the right trajectory!

Problem was, *I* was approaching exhaustion.

Shoes, shorts, t-shirt and all – my gym bag had sat full, at the ready, in the foyer by the front door at the house, for over 8 months. Actually, for the last six, it was tucked away in the adjacent closet; hidden behind the shoe rack – to avoid Melissa's frustrated, but justified, reminders that I should get myself to the gym.

My diet wasn't much better, either. Endless lunches on the road, or with clients, left me with far more extra weight than I'd ever carried in my life; putting more strain on a body whose original long, thin, five-eleven frame wasn't built for that extra pressure, strain, and exertion now needed for basic movement. As a result, my energy level waned, month after month. Three cups of black coffee by noon to get me moving, and conservatively, a couple glasses of wine, to help me wind-down and get some rest at night. Six and a half hours of sleep was considered sleeping-in late, most weekdays.

I knew this lifestyle was not sustainable.

All things considered, Melissa did her best to avoid becoming the nagging partner. But she was genuinely worried, and she had a right to be. My father Robert, passed at a much too young 57 years of age, from a heart attack; and heart conditions run in my family.

Decembers are always a bitter-sweet month for us. We lost

my father on the 3rd; it was a Saturday. He loved and lived the Christmas season, almost as much as a young child, who has yet to uncover the truth about Santa Claus.

Early November 2011, we received our notice of the annual World Trade Center (WTC) Dinner/Celebration, to be held Saturday, December 3rd. Though it had been 9 years since dad passed, Melissa and I had a tradition of spending the first Saturday in December together; doing something fun and frivolous in the afternoon, as a reminder of the light-hearted spirit he brought into a room of family or friends – on any occasion; but even more so at Christmas. And on 'Dad's Saturday', we would cook a meal together, and have a drink by the fireplace after supper, as he and mom often would on winter weekends.

My first reaction to the WTC dinner invitation was to skip it, that year. I knew that it would be encouraging to see many friends, past colleagues; and an opportunity to re-connect with centers of influence I had not seen in quite some time. But most of all, if I did decide to go, it would be to have some time to talk with Pete. He had sent me an email in September, from his cottage somewhere up north in Canada, where he spent all but the winter months of his semi-retirement; having sold – a year after the merger – his share in the firm he founded. I had not spoken to him since my last day at Samson, but now that I look back, the merger with Steadman LLP was no-doubt part of his exit plan, after a long and storied career. That he would be one of the evening's speakers – as an outgoing twelve-year member of the WTC board, and twenty-five-year member of the organization – was further incentive to make the effort to go.

My apprehension was much more than the date of the event. The idea of a quiet, restful evening at home was an enticing alternative. By the time Saturdays rolled around, I was just about out of gas. Since July, our claims business kept growing month over month. And I had made myself a promise, that I would keep up the pace until year's end; re-evaluate where we were, in terms of the overall company; take a good hard look at both business services, and make the necessary changes to bring our lives back into balance. It sounded good. Just the words gave me some temporary relief. But truth be told, I was looking forward to hearing Pete's opinion – some much-needed business and personal perspective beyond me and Melissa – from a person I had great respect for, and trust in.

We decided it would be good for both of us to go. While she did not need more clients, we thought a night of socializing, on a larger scale would be a healthy change to our heavy work schedules. And no doubt she would bump into folks she hadn't seen since college, and her accounting days at KPMG.

We ordered the tickets, and booked a junior suite at the Hyatt Regency for the 3rd, to avoid driving home afterwards, and safeguard against Buffalo's unpredictable, December weather.

We checked-in around three-thirty, unpacked, and kicked-back for a few minutes; side-by-side, on the enormous king bed; before Melissa headed down to the hotel's day-spa, for some well-deserved, and long-overdue, pampering. That was my cue to prep the pillows, and have a short, recovery nap – from a fourteen-hour Friday – that included three out-of-town meetings, and six hours of drive time. The nap felt like ten minutes long. Still, it is amazing what a little shut-eye, a hot shower, and putting on a crisp suit will do for a generally listless state of mind.

We made our entrance to the Grand Ballroom just shy of six-forty-five; collected our seating assignments, and made our way to table twenty-four: near dead-center of the room, about three-quarters of the way back from the center-stage podium. (Perfect, I thought to myself). We introduced ourselves to the table; and after an acceptable period of initial 'get to know you' discussion with the folks seated to my immediate left; I excused myself, having confirmed Melissa's drink preference for the evening; and made my way to the bar.

"Danny!"

That unmistakable, elevated voice – originating from somewhere behind my left shoulder – could only be one person.

As I was about to turn and greet Pete, the bartender sidled along from the gentleman he just finished serving to the right of me. "What will you have sir", he politely asked, while wearing a friendly, yet professional, grin. "Just a minute, please", I replied; while raising one finger, and expressing an understanding, acknowledged look of consideration – that the bar was indeed, busy.

I turned, and spotted Pete in line, about two-suits behind and to the left of me; gave him a nod and a welcoming smile, and asked: "What'll you have Pete, the usual?"

"Sure, if they have it", he replied, with a likewise pleased smile, for his long-time friend.

"Do you have Maker's 46?", I asked?

"Yes, we do sir", he nodded.

"Perfect. A double 'Maker's 46', neat. And… what do you have in single-malt scotch?"

I was surprised to hear a fairly long list of options, and picked one of my favourites: a 15-year old Bowmore, before ordering a Cabernet for Melissa.

Just as the 'house-lights' began to dim, we found a nearby cruiser-table to rest the drinks, and chatted briefly before heading back to our assigned dinner tables. I handed Melissa her Cab', as the wait staff elegantly served our table with appetizers.

"Thanks, honey", she smiled.

"You're welcome, Mel", returning the warm gaze, and planting a slow kiss on her cheek. I had been so wrapped up in business for so long, I had not taken the time to appreciate how beautiful she is, until then: her chestnut brown hair, casually resting on bare, slender shoulders: complements of her new dress; and deep, crystalline-turquois eyes, that appear to go on forever.

"You look stunning, sweetheart", I told her.

"Where did that come from?", she asked playfully.

"It's been far too long, since the last time I told you, how beautiful you are".

"Thanks, honey", she said with a bit of a blush, recognizing that our fellow diners at the table, could not help but overhear our affectionate words.

"You're not so bad looking yourself, ole-man"; her words accompanied by a flirtatious smile; one that I had not seen in quite a while. She loved to tease me about our eight-year age difference. I played along: leaning forward and slightly toward her, extended my right arm out – as if leaning on a cane. In a slow, frail voice, I said: "ahh… what's that, young lady? You will have to speak a little louder"; raising an open, left hand to my ear, simultaneously. She laughed out loud, and then caught herself; recognizing that we were in a conservative setting. Melissa paused… for a few, still-seconds. And then, with an expression that reminded me of the day we met at the UB quad, some seventeen years ago, she said: "You look very handsome tonight, Danny", adding a seductive, subtle wink, for effect.

After dessert, WTC President Craig Tanner, took to the podium for a formal welcome. He thanked the members and guests in attendance, and acknowledged the Mayor, local Senators, and Congress members in the room; along with a number of strong-supporters of the business community, and World Trade Center Buffalo/Niagara.

With his naturally relaxed, yet professional demeanor, Craig gave a warm, respectful, and grateful introduction to Pete, and his Lifetime Contribution Award – the first of its kind, for the organization.

True to form, Pete was relatively-brief, thankful, and appreciative to all those that he worked with in the WTC organization over the years. He shared generous words for his friends, business partners, past employees; and to the community – for giving him the opportunity to have the kind of life, he did not know was possible, as a child. He began to recount the same story, he had privately shared with me about ten years prior: late one Friday, at a local hideaway bar in the Italian quarter of Manhattan, after a conference. I was shocked, and at the same time grateful, for the fortunate upbringing I had in suburban Toronto, compared to his childhood and youth experience, in the small town of Glasgow, Kentucky: population 14,362, as he tells it.

The Grand Ballroom was dead-silent and still, while he spoke. Not just out of respect for the man – what he endured, and what he accomplished – but for his integrity, and his kind-heartedness: those traits remained, no matter how high he rose. But what brought it all home for most, I think, is when he shared his love and appreciation for baseball; as did his brother, Ronnie. Their lives changed, when, at the age of ten – through a sponsored program through the local church – he and Ronnie were invited to play Little League baseball, at no cost to their parents, Dave and Jeannie. All they would need to do is provide cleats for the boys. But there was no money in the Kentucky-based Samson family for an extravagance, like specialty sports shoes; new or used. So, a member of the Glasgow Baptist Church donated a pair of old, weathered, worn down cleats, that were close to the boys' size; allowing the brothers to play on an organized team; that had a coach, took the field at a real diamond, with bases, and a back-drop fence behind home plate. For Peter and Ronnie, it was like being in the big leagues. And it gave them some new-found sense of self-worth.

With one pair of cleats between them – the boys were not able to take the field at the same time in a league game; still, they were ecstatic just to play the national past-time. They made bases out of rocks, used an old borrowed bat and heavily-beaten ball; practising every day, on an abandoned, bulldozed, but unmanaged commercial property, close to the family's home, in the local trailer park. They stuffed newspapers in the toe of each shoe, to make them fit more-properly. And when they practised together, the pitcher-fielder wore the left cleat, while the batter-runner wore the right one; in order to corner the bases, without slipping. Tattered clothing, and two meals a day never bothered the brothers – as long as they had baseball.

At this point in his speech, Pete's eyes began to swell; and the room could feel his unsuccessful effort to hold back the emotion; just as it was in the Manhattan bar that night, ten years prior.

You see, years later, during the last year of high school, both Samson boys accepted full scholarships to the University of Louisville; changing the trajectory of their lives forever…

His brother Ronnie, made it as far as Triple-A ball, with the Louisville Bats. And later, went on to coach the team, before becoming a senior administrator for the International League, based out of Dublin Ohio: where he and his wife Gina now live with their twin boys – whom they now coach, in Little League.

As Pete closed his short speech that night with a quote, I expect I was not the only one to reflect on how lucky I am to have this life. The quote went something like this: "It's not Happiness that brings us Gratitude. It is Gratitude that brings us Happiness."

How right he was.

Just after Craig closed the evening from the podium, I made my way to Pete's table, to congratulate him. By the time I got to the center-front, head table, he was already swarmed by friends and WTC members, offering their appreciation for his words that night; his support over the years, or simply to say: Peter Samson, it has been an honor to know you.

Standing amongst the crowd, Pete caught my eye, and eagerly motioned for me to approach. When I was within ear-shot, he asked: "Danny, can you stick around for while?"

"Of course. I'll come back when it thins out. See you a little later".

"Great", he said, with a thankful smile. And then turned to give his fullest attention to the patient gentleman, now standing directly in front of the man-of-the-evening.

Meanwhile, Melissa was having a great time talking to a small group of UB alumni: some she new personally, others she could relate with shared experiences and fond memories of their college days. I approached cautiously, so as not to interrupt the conversation, but it was too late. Melissa, reached out and took my hand in hers; as she announced to the group: "the best thing about UB, is that's where I met my husband", she said, with an ear-to-ear smile. "Everyone, this is Daniel!", she enthusiastically announced.

I had not seen her so happy since… well, since the days that I was back at Samson LLP. That moment hit me right between the eyes. Three glasses of Cab' didn't hurt, but it was more than that; she was relaxed, playful, and openly conversational in a way I had not seen in a long time. And it was at that instant I realized – that if I had to guess – over the last year especially, about 80% of our discussions had revolved around the firm. (The thought that followed and penetrated the deepest was: we were beginning to lose ourselves, in the business).

I owed it to her; to both of us, to do something about that.

Somewhat distracted, I listened to the stories and updates of the gathered UB clan, now down to six including Melissa; sitting comfortably around a table near the back of the room. The wait staff made their rounds offering a second round of coffee and tea – this time, leaving carafes beside the center-piece. That, and the thinning room, signaled to me that the event was winding down for the evening.

Spotting Pete headed our way, I leaned-in just beyond an ear; letting Melissa know I was going to speak with Pete for a bit. I excused myself, and met Pete half way. We agreed there was time for one more, and headed to the bar, before finding a fairly quiet spot alongside an empty cruiser table.

Pete didn't waste any time. "What's going on, Danny?" he enquired, with a hint of knowing in his tone – that there was something wrong. He knew me well. I wasn't sure if it was my clearly visible weight-gain, or another indicator that I may not have been aware of; though, it really didn't matter.

The best thing about a Peter Samson conversation, is that without saying much of anything, without giving advice or opinions, he helps you to bring the core, important issues to the surface; and you end up recognizing what needs to be done, in order to meet the needs of a situation, yourself. He is a master of asking questions. And that is what he did for nearly an hour. The discussion brought more clarity to some of the necessary changes in my decisions and actions, that would be necessary to bring about progressive improvements to the business, and to our lives. They were little more than reminders, but his timing was impeccable. I had somewhat lost myself, in the business.

He did leave me with a rather abstract perspective, that more or less, summarized an overall error in some of the minor and major decisions we were making.

"Danny, have you ever heard of the term "chasing two rabbits?", he asked.

"Sure. It's a metaphor, that depicts going in two different directions, at the same time… right?"

"That's right. Wanting it both ways, is a more colloquial version of the same meaning", he added. "Where do you see that behavior in your business, and in your life, since opening the firm, and today?", he probed.

"Everywhere!", I laughed, facetiously (but there was some truth to that reactive answer, I realized). "Well, first there are the two services that we offer. I can see that we are hedging our bets."

"And, what do you think is the result?", he queried.

"The result is that my time, my attention, and our resources are pulled in two directions. And, our online marketing message is watered down".

He probed further: "You're right, on all accounts. And those are very important points. But there's an additional effect: look a little deeper. What is your mind forced to do, as a result?"

"It's jumps back and forth, all day long, between challenges and tasks related to the litigation service, and the same for claims service problems: processing, marketing etc.", I conceded.

"Exactly. And from what you've told me so far tonight, you are also shifting between a multitude of tasks, *within* each of those 'business units', throughout your work day. Each time your mind is forced to switch back-and-forth between tasks, it is forced to recalibrate – every time. That tax on your brain is real, and has costs: it takes longer to complete activities, you make more mistakes with decisions and tasks – especially, if they are more complex than trivial. And by the end of the day, you can lose as much as 40% of your productivity by so-called multi-tasking, or 'switching'. Your brain represents only 2% of the body's mass, but consumes 20% of the energy produced by it. That frequent switching of tasks, is likely also costing you money; by way of wasting that much needed energy, to be at your very best, in what you do, each day.

"So… that's likely contributing to my fatigue and lethargy most days?", I posed.

"Sure. And maybe there is more to your energy challenges than 'chasing rabbits' ", he added, with a few shameless, subtle nods.

I got it… clearly.

Pete continued: "You're going to make mistakes, Danny. Transitioning from being an 'attorney' into a 'business owner' was a challenge for me, too. While you may feel 'like a duck out of water' at times, remember: it was that way when you started at the firm… and, what was the final tally of your case record again: 59-0 as 'first-chair'? I've seen 'the lion in you' in the boardroom and the courtroom, when you need to be.

Relax, my friend, you will find your groove."

"Now, tell me about what you are doing online for marketing? And is it making you money, profit?", Pete probed.

"I'm not sure if our online efforts are profitable on their own, but the firm is making a small profit most months, after our salaries. We run Google ads, have a website and blog that have sound SEO, and starting in January, we'll be running Facebook ads. Offline we do print advertising", I explained.

"OK. That's a fairly good start. If you are interested, in the new year some time, I can connect you with my online marketer; he is exceptional; maybe the best there is out there, and he's also a long-time friend."

"Thanks, I appreciate that"; my expression, likely revealing the anticipation inside.
"I didn't know you were involved in online marketing; I heard you were retired, except for a few 'plum' corporate clients?"

"About five years ago, I bought into a relatively small web-based company, on a recommendation from my marketing friend: his name is Joshua Rothsay. The opportunity later arose for us to buy a controlling interest in the business, around the time I sold my share of Samson. After much due diligence on the company and its market potential, Joshua and I negotiated with the principles for 51% ownership; and eventually closed the deal. Everything I have learned about online marketing came from time spent with him. And he has been a trusted, general advisor of mine for twenty-something years now. I owe a lot to him, and he's a sound man; someone I am grateful to call a friend. Just like you, Danny."

"Thanks Pete. You're a good friend, too."

(I could see he was fighting back a yawn, and reasoned it was time to let the 67-year-old get some much-needed rest).

"Must have been a long night for you", I inferred.

"Yeah, it looks like they're about to close the place. What d'ya say we call it an evening?", he suggested.

"Good idea", I replied; both of us already in motion, toward the exit of the Grand Ballroom.

Key Takeaways - Chapter 2

'Mistake #1 – The Four Burners'

The 'Four Burners' metaphor can be a useful way to view your life. I had one burner (work) turned-up 'full-blast', while the others were mostly neglected.

Four Burners: Health and Wellness   Family Relationships
Work and Career   Friends and Fun

I learned the hard way, that it is important for each burner to receive at least their minimal attention, time, and energy. And it turns out, the 'burner activities' tend to 'balance and support' each other.

Please take a moment and reflect on your life conditions. We all neglect to put enough energy into one or more areas of our life.

Recognize, and be ok with that, for now. And if there is a need to make a change, do one new small, simple thing – give the burner(s), a little extra energy…

'Chasing 2 Rabbits'

As you read – in my case, there were a number of 'rabbits' I was chasing. This is a challenge we all have, IMHO.

What I have found to be most-effective, is to remind myself, that *the urge* to 'chase', is the problem; not the 'objects' of the chasing.

For me, the solution has been to recognize in every aspect of life, that it is *never* about 'me'. It is not easy to maintain that perspective, but I have found, that it brings the things that I need, into my life in abundance.

If you are open to an experiment, take a full-day, and approach every aspect of it in terms of the 'other' person(s). Start with relatively unimportant, minor actions and decisions; and see what happens…

CHAPTER 3
One Step Forward, Two Steps Back

It was the coldest January in 57 years. Despite the frigid wind and blustery snow, most mornings I managed to get out for a long walk; though the best I could do within my schedule, was Saturday afternoons, at the gym.

Still, it was a good start.

We surgically trimmed the household and business budgets to make enough room for Cassy coming on-board full-time, five days a week. She started Jan 10th, and by months-end, had taken over 80% of my claims-processing work; freeing up a good-chunk of my daytime to-do-list, and relieving my evening calendar of what was previously, three to four nights a week of burning the midnight oil.

Melissa and I made a pact: every second Saturday would be 'date night'. We put the commitment on our calendars, and agreed to alternate the planning and arrangements. The evening didn't need to be a big event: just dedicated time together, with only two rules: no phones and no shop-talk.

Since neither of us had been on a rink since college, I thought we would both enjoy a night of ice-skating. So, when the temperature eased-off in early February, I dug out the skates and a small knapsack from our sports closet; we layered-up with thermal underwear, sweaters, and ski jackets; and made our way to 'Rotary Rink' – in the heart of downtown Buffalo. Under the warm, nighttime glow of the surrounding high-rise lights, we circled the outdoor ice-pad for about an hour, before I suggested we take a break for some hot cocoa, I'd made before we left the house. Surprisingly, the thermos kept it warm. After watching the skaters glide past for a few minutes, she began to playfully coax and badger me, until I surrendered to playing her favourite game. I'm not sure if it *has* a name, but as in our college dating-days, she subtly identified a person in the crowd, and I had to give that person a name and tell their story – just from their appearance and movements. Being the daughter of a journalist, she was a pro, to my amateur status: her stories often filled with intrigue, adventure, and occasionally scandal. As attorneys do, I would challenge her story: to slow her down, try to trip her up, distract her train of thought when she was on-a-roll. But she always found a way to take the story in another direction; and eventually circled back by the end – addressing most of my 'objections' skillfully: often poking fun at those futile attempts, to throw her off her game.

We laughed a lot that night.

It was only later, while sitting on the sofa – the blazing fire illuminating only its corner of the den – about to pour our first glass of Cabernet; that I realized, we were almost back to our 'old selves'.

By March, I was getting into the groove of my new, more-effective routine. Rather than chasing, and adapting unconditionally to the schedules of litigation prospects, and stacking appointments into any open calendar space – slowly, I was beginning to master maximizing the return on investment of my time. Thanks to my discussion with Pete, I had a new appreciation for the fact that, to be at my best in front of every valuable prospect, I had to be completely clear-headed.

I now recognized that the outcome of my time spent on any business activity was binary: it either produced or contributed to revenue, or it didn't. As a result, I became far more stringent in the qualification of prospects that would warrant an initial meeting; knowing that the 'window' of time that was being invested – and its opportunity-cost – could never be recovered. And my most-important prospect qualification factor shifted – away from '*our* potential revenue' opportunity, to '*their* potential level of benefit': the degree to which they could *and* would benefit from my service to them. As Pete advised, I focussed on uncovering the prospects that most needed my unique skills and experience; they would become referral and testimonial champions of my service, offline and online. I was beginning to see that effect within the first sixty days.

The year-end review of fiscal 2011 uncovered some useful insights. The most noteworthy being the profitability of our claims service: it was *double* that of our litigation clients, after factoring in all related costs. Sure, claims only represented around 25% of our gross revenues, nonetheless, the numbers clearly favored it as the more-lucrative future of the business: it was 'the rabbit' that made most sense to directly pursue. I realized, that it would take some time to effectively, and conservatively, re-deploy our resources; more so, if we were going to make it happen, I needed a plan.

I knew the best way to get Melissa's full buy-in, was with cold, hard numbers. And I had to go through that process anyway, to map out a tactical and financial path toward transition. For the latter half of December, and the first three weeks in January, she had been beginning to take more of an interest: pitching-in to help with my allotment of claims to process in the evening. It didn't take much for her to see the potential: now that she understood the process, saw the current and projected numbers, and recognized the profitability within the expanding system, we had only just begun to build.

At the close of the first quarter, things were beginning to look up for the firm; and our small, three-person team was firing on all cylinders. On a whole, online and offline marketing activities continued to consistently generate leads. Between Cassy, Melissa and me we were assessing, processing, and submitting qualified claims expediently – our straight-forward system was billing approvals within five business days, and converting receivables into cash-in-the-bank within thirty – at a success rate of almost 70%. We were on a roll, and I was beginning to believe we could fully-transition out of the litigation service within 12 to 18 months.

The morning of Friday, April 13th, 2012 – after much back and forth, and three re-scheduling's – I received an email from Pete, committing he and Joshua to meet Monday, May 28th (Memorial Day) at Pete's cottage in Canada. His wife Robyn, suggested Melissa come along, and we could make it into a four-day weekend getaway. Besides Robyn, Joshua's wife Olena would be there on Monday – giving the women an opportunity to relax and catch-up, out of ear-shot from the men's business discussion, that would surely govern most of *our* day. I was eager to learn more about online marketing from an experienced expert like Joshua, and had no-doubt his wisdom would have a significant impact on the rate of the firm's growth: given Pete's endorsement, and what I had learned online about Joshua's numerous success stories.

It was about five months since Pete's offer at WTC; our firm was on a more-solid standing, and moving in the right direction. At long last, I afforded myself a little more optimism over coffee that morning, while continuing to read the remainder of my emails.

Around four-twenty-five in the afternoon, while returning from a meeting in Rochester, my cell rang. Strange, I thought: that Vlad Rimsky would be calling my personal phone; especially this late on a Friday. He was Grayson Inc.'s lead in-house counsel. Other than pre-scheduled conference calls, or in-person meetings, we generally communicated via email. It was unlike him, to call out-of-the-blue, like that. Something big must be going on with the case, I thought to myself, just before answering the call.

Unfortunately, I was right.

"I realize this is rather unexpected, Daniel", Vlad continued; approaching the end of the call. "But Grayson's new senior management were insistent, back in January, that we shift strategy in the direction of a settlement", he added.

"Thanks Vlad, I appreciate the advance notice", I replied; in a confident, secure tone, that in no-way reflected the shock and concern swirling in my head. Over thirty-five percent of our firm's revenue had just evaporated, within the space of a 3-minute conversation, and I had no idea how the company, *and* the household, would survive financially. Melissa had recently referred-out two of her bookkeeping clients to free-up more time for the firm; we had already trimmed our budgets to the bone, to lengthen Cassy's hours, and two-Winter's ago, we took out a 2nd mortgage line-of-credit on the house – initially to keep the business afloat when cash-flow was tight. But the unexpected need to replace our aging furnace *and* the Ford Explorer, drained most of what credit we had been able to squeeze out of our home.

Deep down, I knew there was a viable course through all the obstacles that raced through my mind. Problem was, I could not see anything else.

Pulling off the I-90 early, I headed toward the snow-covered paths of Delaware Park, for a calming walk before heading home to Melissa. One thing was for certain, if we were to find a way through this crisis, my state-of-mind would need to be clear and confident.

As I began to break the news to Melissa over supper, I watched, as an upbeat-smile slowly fell from her face; replaced by one of those deflated expressions: usually worn by people who have lost all hope.

"What happened, Danny? Did you not see this coming?" she asked, (while doing her best to fight back the frustration).

(The past was not going to help us now, I thought to myself). Though I realized, that a fairly thorough explanation would help her bring closure to what had happened. And it was crucial that we quickly move-on to the task of figuring out a game-plan. We both needed to be at our best to tackle what lay ahead.

I explained, "that Grayson 'settling' their class-action lawsuit, with several hundred plaintiffs, was no surprise; though its pre-mature timing, sure was. The company's leadership and management were not directly responsible for the liability in the plaintiffs' complaint, and the entire legal team believed we had a very-strong, legitimate, argument for the 'defense'. But the 'harm' in this case was caused by leaching of toxic chemicals, and many innocent, local residents were likely made ill as a result.

In recent months, local, regional, and national activist organizations somehow got a hold of the community's heart-breaking stories of cancer, birth defects, and alarming rates of various forms of rare illness – resulting in the launch of a massive 'public relations' media campaign.

It was beginning to gain momentum: to sway public opinion – and put pressure on companies like Grayson, who also directly-served the non-commercial, consumer packaging market, as well as multi-million-dollar corporate accounts, that bought and used Grayson products to contain a wide range of consumer house-hold products.

For defendants, cases like these often come down to expense forecast comparisons: 'many years of litigation' versus the 'potential compensation payouts' of a litigation loss. It's just dollars and sense. Grayson shifted to a settlement strategy, in large part, because they were recognizing it was more likely the lesser of two evils for them financially, given the revenue decline they were beginning to see in some product categories already. As *supporting* counsel, our firm was not privy to those high-level, Director and C-suite discussions and decisions".

After answering a few of Melissa's clarifying questions, we sat quietly at the dining-room table for a few minutes. The silence, near-deafening.

Realizing, that nothing had *really* changed yet – a subtle, relieved smile escaped. We would get through this somehow, I thought to myself.

Noticing my renewed facial expression, and more-relaxed posture, Melissa began to mimic the same… and a few seconds later, she matter-of-factly asked: "so, what do we do next?"

Key Takeaways - Chapter 3

'Time is Binary - Unrecoverable'

Pete had me do an audit of the <u>profitability</u> of my time.

He suggested, that a business owner, or any self-employed person, should go through the exercise at least once a year. He emphasized *profitability* over *productivity* – the latter may 'feel' good, he said, but the former is what generates wealth.

(How ironic, my first response was to 'think' that this exercise was not a good use of my time!) If you are open to the process, here are a few of the things Pete suggested I do…

1. Put a dollar figure on the value of your time

2. Using your calendar, phone records, and a daily diary, document everything you do during business hours for at least 1-week, and record (at least) these 3-aspects of each activity:

Category: Admin, Sales, Coaching, Marketing, etc.
New Business Development: Yes/No
Beneficiary: The specific Customer, Prospect, or Campaign

3. Ask: is there another – less-costly – process or person that can perform the task?

'Moving From *Our* Benefit -> To *Their* Benefit'

It sounded obvious to me initially, and I thought we were already 'customer' focussed. But the application of a 'shift' in perspective – from '*our* potential revenue' in an opportunity, to '*their* potential level of benefit', if there were to be a successful sales transaction – was monumental.

The 'shift' changes 'who' is to be pursued and focussed-on, as an 'ideal' prospect.

If done effectively: customizing, branding, and marketing a service more specifically to the 'ideal' client can result in: higher customer satisfaction levels, higher pricing, and a boost to referrals, and online ratings, if you 'work them'.

If that interests you, start with the first things we did: looking at our most satisfied customers, and asking: what traits do 'they' have in common; and what similar consumption and purchase patterns do they display?

CHAPTER 4
The Lake: Part 1
(Website Communication)

Who knew… that at touch-down, a Cessna 206 – landing its aluminium-floats on a choppy, wind-swept morning, would feel like it was hitting a concrete runway – without any landing-gear!

The entire plane, its contents, and us – all shook violently in unison, at the pontoons' first contact with Lake Rosseau. Immediately after impact, the plane rose-up, to about 20-feet above the surging-wake. The lift-sensation, felt somewhat like we were about to take-off again; except for the aircraft's 30-degree left-side-lean: courtesy of an abnormally high, broad-side wave – and what must have been, a severe, simultaneous-gust from the south-west. I reactively glanced-over at Pete, looking for some reassurance, that he was in control of the plane: as it flew off-kilter, for what seemed-like at least a hundred yards or so. The expression on my face must have given-away the concern, along with an incoherent sound that resembled some combination of the words: "wow" and "ahh!". The near-screams from the wives, seated immediately behind us, were a less-subtle signal, of *their* surprise and terror.

"We're ok!", Pete abruptly exclaimed.

But his stern expression, stiff posture, and tightly-clenched hands – gripping the 'stick', indicated otherwise.

Out of instinct, he leaned slightly to the right, while trying to level-out the plane's 'roll', and to avoid further 'banking' to the left. The adjustment was mostly successful, but we were still in an awkward, upward 'pitch' – that even I could tell, was too steep for a safe landing. As we began to descend again, Pete adjusted the 'flaps'; settling the aircraft into perfect posture just as it hit the water for touch-down #2. This one, thankfully, a brief, far-less-severe, 5-second bounce-lift-and-fall, peaking at about 10-feet above the water's surface. Like a stone skipping across a pond – the Cessna bounced twice-more, before the pontoons finally planed relatively-smoothly, across the choppy lake. Then, we quickly decelerated-down, over an eighty-yard stretch, to a comfortable 15-knots.

"Ladies and gentleman, welcome to Lake Rosseau; local-time is 11:47am", Pete half-sarcastically announced through our in-flight intercom-headsets, as we began to slowly 'taxi' toward the south-west shoreline.

Barely fifteen-minutes later; having just de-planed – a large duffle-bag slung over my shoulder – I was never so-relieved, to be standing on solid, dry, ground again. Based on the silence of the others, it was fairly certain, that *I* wasn't the only thankful-one, that morning.

We all stretched, and took a few deep breaths dock-side; taking in the lake and its natural surroundings, before the significant, upward stair-climb to the cottage.

What impressed us most, about the Samson's 3,200 square-foot, chalet-style, Summer home overlooking the lake, was the extra care and cost invested, to preserve the integrity of its original foliage and tree line, surrounding the structure. Other than a forty-foot clearing, that enabled a view of the lake, from the large, second-floor, A-framed living-room – the intrusion of 'man' into nature's domain was kept to the barest of minimums.

After unpacking our gear for the weekend, the four of us met-up in the living-room. Pete and Robyn shared some stories of their most-recent winter, down-south; and we all caught-up, on local happenings back in Western New York, since the Samsons' departure from the region. When the ladies' side-bar conversation started to steer toward local gossip, Pete and I agreed, that ninety-minutes-past-noon was an acceptable time to crack a cold one, and move our chat outside to the second-floor balcony, that spanned the cottage's central A-f rame.

"So, how're you and Melissa and the business doing, Danny?", he asked, while twist-opening the first Molson Canadian of the day.

I followed his lead; then raised, and slightly-tipped my bottle, adding "cheers", to buy myself a few seconds. The last thing I wanted to do, was start the conversation with all of the challenges we were currently facing; nonetheless, I knew Pete would genuinely want to hear, and help, where he could.

"The claims-service business was growing, and it was decidedly the future of the business", I explained. "Losing Grayson earlier than expected, last month, was a big-blow to our cash-flow, and would, next-month, put us seriously in the red: given that their previous and final billing was May 1st". I went on to outline our cost-cutting plan. "Reluctantly, we had reduced Cassy's hours back to two and a half days-a-week; and she was not happy. We sold the 2011 'Explorer', and replaced it with a smaller, 2003 'Escape'. We took 'a bath' on the transaction, but pocketed $15,300 in cash to give us more 'runway'. I had known our office building's landlord, Jacob Martins, for fifteen years, and was able to negotiate a three-month rent-payment 'holiday' in return for an equal-term lease-extension, plus a 'personal guarantee'. We determined which of our business and household bills could be extended to a 45-day payment cycle over the next three months; and reduced or eliminated any expenses that were not critical to the business and our basic living needs. Our revised budgets were laid-out in QuickBooks, and Melissa was the oversight 'hawk' to keep us on-plan. It was all based on 90-day re-evaluation cycles, and predicated on our confidence in incremental revenue growth of the 'claims' business".

"That's where you and Joshua, come in", I added; offering Pete an opportunity to provide his input.

"It sounds like you and Melissa have done a thorough job evaluating your options, and trimming as many expenses as possible", he began. "I have some good news about Joshua. We spoke late last night, and it appears that he'll be able to spend more time with us, this weekend. His wife Olena, is not able to make the trip up to Rosseau until Monday morning. Their cottage is also on Rosseau, a little north of us, up the shoreline. Joshua has been up here since Wednesday, working on his new book. We'll see him around 4 today, and he'll be staying for dinner.

"That *is* good news", I said, and added: "I'm looking forward to meeting him. Is everything alright with his wife?"

"Olena's fine. She had to stay a few extra days in Miami, for the opening of her latest Spa. Smart lady… I think this is her seventh location. Robyn and I don't get to see her much, I hope she can make it up here Monday… she is a lot of fun. You'll like her, Danny".

"Sounds like it", I replied.

Pete continued: "with your business, three months is a short window to make significant strides in results with online *or* offline marketing; especially if you have limited resources. But, if there's anyone who can help you turn-around the business in short-order, it's definitely Joshua", he added.

"Well, Melissa and I are grateful for your invitation, and the introduction. It could not have come at a better time", I replied.

There would be plenty of time to talk-shop about 'the firm' later, I thought. I asked Pete how he was enjoying semi-retirement, and the conversation meandered over the next few hours, as he showed me around the property, and shared some stories of the many functions he and Robyn had hosted there, over the previous two decades.

Around twenty-to-four, we headed down to the dock to await Joshua's expected early arrival. As Pete had explained, he would be early by at least ten minutes. True to form, we could see the 32-foot 'Sea-Ray Sundancer' approaching; its' long, sleek bow cutting across the wake – now somewhat more settled than earlier that morning. Pete had been a follower of Joshua's philosophy on appointment-timing, for many years, and it made sense to me too.

Since his early days selling insurance, as Joshua had described it to Pete, "if a prospect, or a person, had made a commitment of their time to see him at their office or home, they have a degree of interest in purchasing something, or sharing some of their finite personal time, in the case of a social meeting". Pete continued: "selling is hard work; and the last thing you want to do Danny, is diminish their interest with something as easy as managing *your* time, in order to arrive on-time. Fundamentally, being late is a disrespect; or rather, it can send the message that your time somehow has more value than theirs. The higher you go up the food chain, so to speak, the more aware folks are of those subtle cues: indications of where *your* perspective is, within the business transaction that they are considering with you.

"huh, I hadn't looked at it that way before", I commented.

"It's more than that Danny. In business, by not showing up early, you can miss out on the opportunity of learning something valuable on-site, before the meeting. Joshua taught me early-on, that I should target my arrival time 30-minutes before the appointment, to account for any last-minute minor or major delays on-route. More importantly, with an early arrival, you can use that time to observe and learn as much as you can about the company: from its exterior, interior, and any staff or management you may come into contact with. For more than twenty-five years, I was sure to be at the receptionist's desk promptly, fifteen minutes before every appointment. More often than not, my appointee would be notified that I was there, waiting for him or her, *early*. And it's amazing what you can learn, and who you might end-up talking to unexpectedly. Sometimes those interactions impact the trajectory of a sales-call or the business transaction you are pursuing. Consider them as bonuses: gifts that can't be received, if you don't show up early, Danny."

I had not yet met Joshua, and already I was impressed by his attention to the subtle details. Pete told me that in his experience, it's the aggregation – of many, small, uncovered insights – that when put into action, differentiate 'exceptional' performance and results, from merely 'good'.

I gave that one a few moments to settle, before recognizing its logical relationship to success...

"Danny, can you grab the bow-line?" Pete's requested, as Joshua's sleek Sea-Ray, slowly gurgled its way into the guest 'slip', adjacent to the boathouse.

" Pete, how the heck are ya!", were Joshua's first words, as he stepped onto the dock, and gave his friend a firm, jovial handshake.

"Living the dream Josh, how're *you*, old man!", replied Pete; adding a 'good-ole-boy' Kentucky belly-laugh, that near shook the dock.

"This youngster, was born fifteen-years before me, and still calls me old man!", Josh countered, giving Pete an admiring slap on the back, while joining in the laughter.

"Josh, this is Danny, the friend from New York I told you about".

"Danny, good to meet you!", said Josh, while shaking my hand; still somewhat amid laughter.

"Good to meet you, Joshu-", before finishing, his friendly interruption stopped my words mid-sentence.

"Call me Josh, Danny. From what Pete has told me about you, we'll likely be fast-friends. And besides, there's no need for formality; *especially here*": turning his gaze slightly, to show his appreciation for the picturesque, Muskoka scenery.

Our entrance interrupted Robyn and Melissa, still fully-engaged in conversation, while preparing the salad, and cutting vegetables for supper. Pete introduced Josh to Melissa, and Robyn gave him a warm-welcome hug: the type reserved for two long-time, close friends. A few catch-up discussions later, Robyn asked about Olena's delayed return from Miami; and finished with a proposed agreement, that Melissa and she had worked-out before making their way to the kitchen, a-half-hour earlier.

"Gentleman, we decided to make supper tonight, on the condition that you guys take double-duty Saturday and Sunday", she said; in a friendly, half-proposing, half-insisting tone.

"Sold!" Pete and I responded in unison; pleased that we could head-down to the roof-top boathouse patio, for another 'Canadian' or two, before supper.

"Dinner's at six, Robyn kindly reminded – the three men already on our way through the exterior sliding- glass doors, that led to a wrap-around deck, surrounding three-quarters of the Samson summer home.

(It's a much easier walk downward, I thought to myself, as we made our way toward the lakeside boathouse, that Pete often used for smaller, outdoor social functions).

Pete pulled three cold-ones from the bar-fridge, along with frosted mugs that he kept chilled in its freezer. Josh and I sat comfortably on stools, watching as Pete carefully poured and served our Canadians on a coaster, like an attentive, professional bartender would. The conversation eventually made its way around to 'the firm'. (Though admittedly, I was enjoying my brief vacation from the topic of business just fine, until then).

"How is the business, Danny?", Josh asked.

After an explanation of the last few months challenges, and an outline of our already 'in-play' plan of action, Josh focussed-in on business development; specifically, our online marketing and the results it was producing.

"Attribution is a common challenge for most companies, Danny. You are not alone with that one. But knowing which marketing activities produce results, is a necessary component to scaling-up your service nationally. But we can come back to 'attribution' later, Let's start with your website".

Josh continued, "your website, especially the home page, is like the exterior of your house, if you were in the process of selling it. Potential purchasers drive-by a home for sale in neighbourhoods they like, and gather an initial impression; the same holds true for online viewers, surfing the web for homes to purchase. The interior may have a superb-layout; be extremely family-friendly and functional, energy-efficient, and come with all the amenities that a specific type of buyer would want; but if the 'front-end' does not reasonably reflect the interior 'substance' – the seller risks the home being passed-over early in the buyer's 'search' phase. The viewer will relate to the style of the exterior, as kindred to who they are, or otherwise; even if it is presentable and clean".

"Make sense so far?", Josh queried.

"Yes, I'm with you. We need to shift our home-page message, to be dominated by our claims-processing service", I replied.

"That's not news to you, I understand. It is sometimes easier and more effective to work with an analogy when trying to solve our own challenges. There are many similarities with marketing your service online, and residential property.

If you don't mind, we'll continue with some basics that you may already know, and progress into the lessor-known, tactics, after that. It all fits together.

Are you alright with that?", he asked.

"Absolutely", I replied. "I have a question, though… what is the difference between a landing-page and the home page? Are they the same thing?

"Good question, Danny. Think of your website as an entire book, and the landing-page is a single-page within that book. If someone types in the URL of your website: davidsonfirm. com, they will land on your home page. In that case, *it's* considered the 'landing page'. However, if they use specific keywords in Google or another search engine, they may initially land on another page within your website – one that contains content most-directly related to that keyword search. In that scenario, *its* the landing-page. With an online marketing campaign using Google Adwords or Facebook advertising, for example, you would direct 'click-throughs' of your ad to a target web-page, often custom-created for the campaign. In that case, the website location where they are intentionally re-directed to, we call the landing-page. We'll go through more on landing-pages later, but does that answer your question, for now?

"Yes, it makes sense", I confirmed.

"Ok, good. I spent some time this morning reviewing your website. Most websites have a lifespan of 3 to 5 years; we do a site review for our clients', every two years, to keep them current. For the most part, yours has the main content components covered. What needs some work, is the flow of your 'messaging' to the prospect. In other words, the reader should be directed through your website, via a pre-planned 'path'. Scrolling a well-constructed 'path', the viewer should be unconsciously 'checking-off' in their mind, the resistance points that are necessary to be overcome, before they will take a next-step action: one that is closer to engaging your service.

My approach is not unique; many marketing firms use it, or something similar, within their communication strategy. It is the skill-full application that separates 'exceptional' website paths from 'good' ones. In fact, this fundamental knowledge that many of us use, is about 2,300 years old; coined by the ancient Greek philosopher Aristotle. His art of persuasion was based on three principles: Ethos, Pathos, and Logos.

Ethos is all about building trust, credibility, and character. On *your* website, you ask the prospect, early in their navigation process, to fill-in a 'free evaluation' form, which includes some of their personal information. I see that as the engagement-objective, that the entire site is working toward. The question is, at what point in their information gathering, are they comfortable sharing personal data? If we could view in real-time the behavior of visitors to your site, we would see exactly where they are dis-engaging, what their pattern of movement within the site looks like; where they pause, where they scroll-read un-interruptedly, and so on. Knowing the 'bounce' points on your website, is invaluable for making the right adjustments to your content, layout, or navigation strategy (the 'website path'). When we know that your website has instilled trust and credibility, you are one-step closer to engagement. If there is time, we will walk through how you can 'view' prospects' behavior on your website.

Pathos is the awakening of emotion in the website reader-visitor; sufficiently for them to 'want' what you have to offer. While you are offering a service, the potential buyer also wants to know that you understand their problem; and that you empathize sufficiently with their situation: most feel that their situation is unique. In the sales process, you are attempting to persuade the prospect on two levels: *first*, is the 'role' that they play in the transaction. If the purchase is a commercial product or service, the decision-maker is playing the role of 'President', or maybe they are the 'Marketing Manager', a 'Compliance Officer', or 'Purchasing Manager'. There are responsibilities they must meet in that 'role'.

Secondly, is the person: the 'human-being' beneath the role. And the same holds true in a 'consumer' purchase transaction. The prospect may be playing the role of 'parent' if the purchase is for a child; a 'son' or 'daughter', in the case of a product or service bought by a parent. It is important to recognize that in your communication to prospects, both 'self-identifications', whether conscious or not, need to be addressed, if you want to persuade them to engage at the next level, and ultimately, to make a purchase.

The bonus by-product of going through the process of identifying the traits and behaviors associated with each 'role', is that you will come to understand and empathize with the 'human-being' and the 'role-player', and this will instill you and your process with a deeper sense of integrity and authenticity. If the prospect is not a good 'fit' for your product or service, they will naturally not purchase or engage further online – which is what you want: a sales funnel filled with *qualified*, *interested* buyers. With a personal, direct-selling interaction, you can choose the direction to take a conversation in real-time. Hopefully, you agree that letting an unqualified buyer 'off the hook', is in everyone's best interest.

A forced, 'persuaded-sale' generally ends up costing time and money for all parties involved, and is the cause of most dis-satisfied, complaining clients down the road.

Related to Pathos, the question to ask yourself in your claims business, is what are the underlying emotions present in prospects before they engage your service, and what are they likely to be after a successful approval: when they receive the monetary award? My understanding of your potential prospects, is that they may be the 'actual worker' that was made-ill by the job they performed; they may be the surviving spouse or children; or they may even be the surviving grandchildren. Each group may or may not have

63

similar motivations to pursue a claims-case; though it will be some mix of 'monetary' and 'emotional'.

If your website communication comes close to a mix that matches your prospects, you are on the way to having a 'winning website'".

"Are you still with me, Danny?", Josh checked-in.

"Yes, it all makes sense. This is really helpful. It already sounds like we have a lot of work to get into, back at the office", I acknowledged.

"I understand. Stay with me, Danny. I have a content expert that will help you with the process".

"Ok", I confirmed.

"Equally necessary in sales and marketing, is **Logos**: Aristotle's third persuasion-principle: the appeal to reason and logic. Many marketers and business owners rely too heavily on this one, mostly in isolation of the other two. Facts, analogies, and logical arguments appeal to one's deeper sense of 'reason'. You may see some perceived cross-over between Ethos and Logos: the difference is that Ethos builds the case for the character: credibility and trust-ability of the author or salesperson; while with Logos, *the rationale* of a well-reasoned and supported argument, stands on its own.

For a website to 'hit it out of the park' consistently, its content must contain a skill-full application of all three persuasion-principles".

Pausing for about twenty seconds, Josh continued; with a question: "what are you thinking, Danny?"

"My first instinct is that we should re-build the website. While that may be the longer-term best direction, the short-term focus of my time is to generate more clients, within the next 90-days. Given our current financial situation, where do you suggest we start, Josh?

"Well, while you are here at the cottage this weekend, bare in mind that over the next three days, you will be exposed to a lot of relevant, helpful reminders; as well as new information. At times, you may feel an urgency to act – which is a good thing. I am here to help you, and I have a team of experts in the application areas that you will need. 'The Davidson Firm' is *your* company, and it is important that its communication, like the website, reflect who you are, and how you choose to serve your clients. That way, the messaging carries with it an integrity and authenticity, that no outside marketing company can create, independent of your input and participation. We'll work together, to address your short-term needs, and longer-term strategic vision for the firm. There is much still to share with you, and it is important to recognize, that your current challenges will pass. I have been through the business and personal obstacles that you are facing now, and I know what it takes to persevere, make the appropriate, necessary changes, and to be open to what is still to be learned.

I would not have agreed to work with you, if I did not know that you have the character and drive to build a great company".

"Are you ready to continue on, Danny?"

"Absolutely… let's do it!", I replied.

Key Takeaways - Chapter 4

'The Art of Persuasion – Ethos, Pathos, and Logos'

Through a website audit with Josh and his team, we discovered that our website was informative, but had a lot of room for improvement, related to Aristotle's persuasion principles:

Ethos is all about building trust, credibility, and character.

Pathos is the awakening of emotion in the website reader-visitor; sufficiently for them to 'want' what you have to offer.

Logos: is the appeal to reason and logic.

If your website is due for a content audit, related to its persuasive power; consider classifying all of the content, into one of these three principles: Ethos, Pathos, and Logos. If your website's persuasion efforts are well-covered, balanced, and thorough, you can 'check-off' all three areas... as will your prospects!

'Show Up Early!'

There are three benefits that I discovered, after following Josh's practise of showing up early:

1. Something new about the company was learned just by paying close attention to the exterior and interior of their premises. It generally reflected the leadership, or ownership of the organization.

2. On occasion, I have been accepted into a sales appointment early. I don't know about you, but I appreciate any extra time I can spend with a prospect… I consider it bonus time, that I would not have had.

3. More often than not, a conversation ensues with a representative of the company, and I take that opportunity to learn something about the business, that I did not know beforehand.

Try it for a week, and see what happens…

CHAPTER 5
The Lake: Part 2
('Search-Engine Marketing')

Glancing first at his watch – Josh replied, "ok"; while nodding his acceptance of Pete's visual-offer of a second beer, before dinner. I wasn't sure where Josh would take the discussion next, but I knew that it would lead to more learning, additional perspective about my business, and useful advice we could act on, back at the office.

"How familiar are you with 'Search-Engine Marketing' (or SEM), Danny", he asked; gauging my knowledge, for where to go from there.

"Well, I think our marketing vendor did a fairly good job of explaining how Google Adwords and Facebook advertising work. We promote our claims-service on both platforms, and it appears as though they are bringing in leads, so far", I responded.

"Ok. Did they explain, or offer a strategy for transitioning your budget and resources over time, to increase the results from your 'organic' search-engine marketing?", he enquired.

"Not really. They said they would continue to improve our

'search engine optimization' (SEO) over time, and that service is included in our monthly fees; in addition to Adwords and Facebook Ad spending", I replied.

"Alright. Do you mind if we spend our remaining time before supper, on 'organic' versus 'paid' online marketing?", he offered.

"Of course, I'm all ears", I replied.

"Great. Let's go back to our analogy of residential property. But this time, reflect back on the time you and Melissa rented your first apartment together; before you purchased your home. This might sound like an obvious question, but what motivated you-two to save for your own home?", asked Josh.

I explained that "our parents instilled in both of us, the value of owning our own home; of buying as early as we could, in order to start building-up equity. We knew that our monthly rent payments were providing us a current benefit – a roof over our heads – but we would not see any future return, and would be stuck in that cycle of paying rent our entire lives. It was not easy to pay rent and save for a house, but the sacrifice, and investment in our future, was well worth it".

"Exactly. To understand the fundamental difference between Google's 'paid' versus 'organic' *lead-generation opportunities*, think of your Google Adwords budget as regular rent payments. You are temporarily renting virtual space, on their platform: in essence, Google is your landlord. An important difference to recognize, is that with 'real property' rent, you have a lease, and the rent payments are equal and consistent. Adwords' 'virtual rental space' cost is 'on-demand', within the framework of a continuous bidding system, that is (loosely) based upon three factors:"

1. Your ability to pay the 'rent' for each and every visitor to your website
2. Your ability to 'out-bid' your competitors
3. Your Quality Score

"We will walk-through Quality Score a little later, Danny".

"Since you appreciate the value of 'ownership' over 'renting'; let's contrast 'paid' Adwords with an effective 'organic' search-marketing strategy. Since nearly 63% of online searches are made through Google, I will refer to them specifically; though the strategy I use, is effective for all search-engines (24% Bing and 12% Yahoo!, the other 1% are small search engines).

Most companies use Adwords to generate leads, as a result of not having the capability to capture high-organic-ranking, for their own website pages. Remember, that each 'page' on the internet, is individually indexed by the search engines; so, in effect, you already *own* a number of, what I refer to as 'on-website' – 'content-properties'. What we will be doing together, is developing a significant volume of high-quality, one-page websites that do not reside on your main website. These 'content-properties' will be, in effect, a portfolio of 'virtual real-estate'.

An effective 'content-property' strategy, is planned and created around your service's most relevant 'Subject Categories': those areas of interest, that potential purchasers, and target information seekers, are most likely to look for, online. The distinction is that over time, you will *own* content that 'ranks' high in organic search; and become less and less dependent on 'renting' non-recoverable, impermanent space from Google. More so, a well-developed content-property portfolio can provide you the visibility benefits of multiple 'page' ranking exposure, from a single 'search' made by folks seeking a vendor, or service provider like you. A content-property strategy, can be 'Geo-Targeted' to appear in local, regional, national or global searches, depending on the scale you want your online 'reach' to be.

 If you were to tackle the development of 'content-properties' on your own Danny, these are the general components, or key competencies required, to build high-ranking 'organic' content:

1. A deep understanding of the criteria that Google uses to 'rank' their organic search-results

2. An understanding of the 'Subject Categories' (SC's) most relevant to your target prospects

3. An ability to develop SC content that is unique and educational to the person searching, *and* is effective at 'ranking' high – because a search engine also recognizes that it be educational and unique. This is referred to as writing for Search Engine Optimization or 'SEO writing'.

That you have already identified a substantial niche-service, leads me to believe that yours can not only be an extremely lucrative national business; but, relatively quick, short-term results are probable. My clients, most in more-crowded categories, are able to build significant 'organic' exposure. If we invest in the right mix and quantity of 'content properties' for your firm – along with the other tactics I will soon be sharing with you" – in a year or so, you will dominate your online category.

Josh paused for a moment, realizing that we were likely approaching the six-o'clock dinner-hour commitment, we had made to Robyn and Melissa.

"What questions do you have so far, Danny?", he asked.

"I'm curious to hear your perspective on Google's Quality Score. But it can wait till after dinner", I conceded.

With a subtle chuckle and a pleased smile, he said: "you

are one-step ahead of me, Danny. It's good to hear you are grasping the logic, and looking ahead to the next steps".

Pete, chimed-in, half-laughing his words, while clearing and tucking the empties temporarily behind the bar: "Hey Josh, we're late for dinner, it's ten to six!"

"I timed the stair-climb up to the cottage years-ago! We'll be there with seven minutes to spare", Josh countered, then added: "ah, well, at least *Danny and I* will get there on time... I'm not so sure about you, old man!", slapping his friend on the shoulder, for effect.

The three of us laughed out loud – likely more boisterously, than we would have, without a few late-afternoon beers – and began our walk down the boathouse stairs, and up to the cottage.

After dinner, Pete lit a fire, and the five-of-us gathered on the over-sized, L-shaped, living-room sofa, that faced the lake. After about forty-minutes of casual conversation, Josh indicated that he should make his way back to his cottage, before the sun fully-set, within the hour. He needed to spend a few hours on his book; and as a precaution, preferred not to dock the big 'Sundancer' in the deep darkness of a Muskoka night. Pete jokingly 'gave him the gears' about leaving the party early; before relenting his understanding, and thanking Josh for sharing his time with us. I appreciatively said the same, and shook his hand, before Melissa and Robyn wished

74

him their warm 'good-nights'.

"Do you mind giving me a hand with 'casting-off' the boat, Danny?", Josh asked.

"Sure", I replied; knowing his likely motivation was to finish the day's discussion, about search-marketing.

Down on the dock, we found two Muskoka chairs, already well-positioned for conversation, and with a bonus view of the partially sun-lit, Tobin Island shoreline.

(There was a question on my mind that needed to be answered, before I moved too far forward, assumptively, about how I would compensate Josh for the wealth of knowledge he was sharing, and the practical-application-help, he had fore-mentioned a few times, so far).

"Josh, thank you for being so generous with your time, to help us. I know that you're familiar with our financial situation, and yet it's important to Melissa and I to repay you in some way. Have you had clients like us in the past?", I inferred.

"I understand, Danny. Years ago, I was in a similar position with a business. I was forced to sell my company. We won't let that happen to you. I respect your intention to balance the transaction. There are three scenarios that come to mind. I have worked similarly in the past, with one individual, and what I proposed to him was that we could work out a future payment amount and schedule, based on the success of his firm; or he could simply 'pay-it- forward', when he himself, had gained mastery of the principles and tactics. Or, when the opportunity arose, he could refer me a client, if he believed they were a good fit for my business.

Lastly, he could choose any combination of those. But with you, I thought of a fourth option, for your consideration. As you know, I am writing a book, to help business owners gain a clearer understanding of online marketing; and what they can do to accelerate the growth of their companies. The nature of *your* business would make an excellent case study. If you are open to that, it is also a compensation option. If you choose the last option, I would of course, change your names and circumstances somewhat, to protect your anonymity. There is no need for you to make a decision now; we can talk about that after you and Melissa have had a chance to discuss. I am comfortable moving forward now with our working together, if you are?"

"Thanks Josh, those options are all very generous. I am all-set to continue, now that I know we'll be repaying you in some form".

"Perfect. We were discussing organic and paid search-marketing, before dinner. And I believe we were about to move into Google's 'Quality Score'. Is that right?", he asked.

"Yes", I replied.

"Ok. For context, let's combine 'Quality Score' with a discussion on the concept of 'transition' – from your company's current focus of 'paid' advertising, to a more 'organically-driven' lead-generation 'system'. To understand the most effective path through a marketing/business 'transition', we first need to take a step-back from sales and marketing; and examine for a moment, what 'business' actually is, fundamentally. What is beneath the concepts that we refer to as: sales-calls and campaigns, meetings and roles, and the physical processing of functions, such as: order-taking; invoicing and billing; the components of producing a product, or the steps involved in the fulfillment of a service: online or offline. What is *actually* going-on within an organization?

Beneath it all Danny, is simply 'activity'.

That is all a business actually is.

The majority of that 'activity', leaves behind evidence of itself, in the form of data. And using today's technology, the lion's share of that online and offline 'activity' can now be captured, analyzed, and utilized by you, to make better sales and marketing decisions. This is known today as "Data Analytics." It empowers you, with a perspective that approaches your being physically present in all areas, and to view from an outside perspective, the 'activity' that occurs within your business: the causes and effects that produce favourable and unfavourable results.

Think of it like a 'window' into your business, Danny, that you yourself, are not able to entirely see – because you are a part of it.

With that additional knowledge, perspective, and understanding in hand, we will be able to create manageable sales and marketing 'systems'; which I understand, is what you are interested in building.

"Danny, are you familiar with W. Edwards Deming?", he asked.

"The name sounds familiar", I replied.

Josh continued: "Deming is credited with being the pioneer of Total Quality Management, and is most notable for going to Japan in the 1950's as a consultant, at a time when the country was known for its inferior, cheap, low-quality products. His *original* philosophy is based on the continuous improvement of systems and processes, and is held-up as a major reason Japanese manufacturing re-invented itself, into a worldwide, leading producer of quality products. Its exports of automobiles and electronics fueled an economic boom for the country, and the accomplishment spearheaded others to adopt Deming's 14-step method for superior output and quality. The methodology underlies management, marketing, and innovation principles found within today's tech icons and various industry leading companies. At the core, it is best summarized in his famous quote:

Without data, you're just another person with an opinion.

His contemporary: Presidential Medal of Freedom winner and marketing management thought-leader Peter Drucker, echoed Deming, and influenced the modern marketing era; most notably, with his similar philosophy, captured succinctly in his quote:

What gets measured, gets managed.

These exceptional innovators and thinkers, have had a deep-influence on my success over the years, and their teachings are the foundation of what is referred to as 'evidence-based marketing'. Google's Quality Score is an example of 'evidenced-based-analysis'; the opposite side of what we will be doing with your firm's sales and marketing data. The Quality Score is derived by analyzing three aspects of an Ad:

1. The Expected Click-Through Rate of your Ad

2. The Relevance of Your Ad, to the target keywords that you are using

3. Landing Page Experience – the likelihood a viewer will be satisfied with your page's information

To develop a high 'Quality Score', you must use the same method as building effective-ranking content-properties: a combination of A/B testing, along with the deployment of Aristotle's principles of Ethos, Pathos, and Logos, to craft an Ad and Landing Page, that gains the viewers attention, elicits engagement, and invokes a deep desire – to take a directed, guided 'action'. The process is straight-forward; but not easy to execute-well. Fortunately for you and me, I have an experienced team, that has worked with content and online marketing for almost two decades now.

The core concept behind both Google's Quality Score algorithm, and a component to our exceptional online results, is 'attribution': the determination of *influential activities or factors* that cause a response, or an outcome. With Google's 'Page' rank and 'Quality Score' algorithms, they are correlating factors that indicate a favourable online experience has/will occur, for folks in 'search' mode, online. While no one knows the exact number, Google's organic search indexing algorithm is estimated to incorporate over two hundred 'attribution' factors; some of which are obvious and logical – like engagement time spent on a page or website, web-page loading time, user interaction, and how frequent content is updated. We have discovered, through extensive A/B testing over many years, well-over one hundred of the attributes, that directly affect ranking: that is why I am confident we will develop content for your firm, that will rank highly.

One of the main reasons 'online-based' businesses vastly outpace traditional 'offline' businesses, is that they have a much deeper appreciation and understanding of 'attribution'. As a result, they can make more-effective changes, and quicker.

They satisfy customers at a much higher level of success, and grow many times faster, because decision-makers are empowered with a robust collection of information, that more-closely reflects reality – of the challenges they are attempting to solve, and the customers they are diligently working hard to serve, and highly-satisfy. The reason I work exclusively with small-cap companies (under $50M in revenue) like yours, is because they are more agile than their larger counterparts; and most are free from the bureaucracy and politics that limit their ability to make shifts and transitions at a brisk pace. They are akin to a chugging 'Titanic' as compared to my responsive 'Sea-Ray Sundancer'. Current technology, Danny, gives smaller businesses the advantage – if they are like you: open to seeing its possibilities; and its inevitability.

I realize this is rather abstract, Danny. But does it make sense to you?"

"It sounds logical, so far", I replied.

"Alright. Let's relate 'attribution' now, to your online 'search marketing' transition from Adwords to 'organic' results, using 'content-properties'.

There can be a dual-purpose to Adwords campaigns. Many companies – (hopefully, including your marketing vendor) use A/B testing, or 'split-testing' – to gauge which Subject Categories (or areas of interest to the target prospect) produce the most click-throughs (CT's) to a landing-page –

by comparing the results of two or more ads. They then run more ads with the 'winning' Subject Categories until the click-through-rate (CTR) declines, or they uncover other 'test' ads, that produce superior results. While that process validates their service fees, there are a number of important 'analysis gaps' that can be missed. Let's go through a few of them now, and then we will walk-through an alternative methodology.

1. Ad Keywords that produce an elevated CTR are not necessarily <u>profitable</u> ads.

2. Ad Keywords that produce a 'click-to-action (CTA), like an enquiry, are not necessarily <u>profitable</u>.

3. Ad Keywords that decline in CTR, or are eclipsed by another, can still be <u>profitable</u>.

The only metric that *really* matters, in a marketing campaign, is its profitability. In other words, does that ad return 1.x or more of the investment? You can't pay the bills, or yourselves, with any of the various other statistics or analytics reported from online activities. This is why mastering 'attribution' is so important.

The challenge is that you must first consolidate your 'online' and 'offline' data, if you want to be able to accurately correlate which activities generate profit, and to what degree. Remember, our goal is the ROI of every marketing dollar you spend. We will do this early in our working relationship, so that you will have a clear view of profitability. And you will quickly see that mastering 'attribution' is a huge competitive advantage."

"Danny, do you have any questions about attribution?"

"No, it makes sense. And I can see how important it is to our growth rate".

"Ok, good. Another important function in any ongoing marketing activity, is to establish a 'baseline' of results. Baseline is the average of the metric that is being measured. For example, if you run five different test ads, over a week, and the average daily click-through is 187; ads that are producing less than 187 CT's should be discontinued; assuming all ads are equally profitable. An ad that is producing above the baseline of 187, should be continued indefinitely. In our example, if 3 of 5 ads are above baseline, we would replace the two 'losing' ads, with fresh ads, and once again test for a week, or longer, depending on the budget and the nature of what is being sold.

Since we are learning, and improving each successive ad, the next test should produce a baseline average greater than 187; say 193. That becomes our 'new baseline', and we simply continue to follow the same process. This is, as I am sure you can see, an example of Deming's 'continuous improvement'. The result, is that the *rate* of revenue and profit increase, *rises* consistently over time. It is important to recall that you are 'playing a long game', in business, Danny. A continuously improving system, as you know, is how significant future growth, profit, and wealth are derived, in business.

There are additional methods that we use to determine the basis of what should be included in a content-property. If we have time later this weekend, we can go through those together.

It is important to remember, that most people still choose 'organic' listings over 'paid ads', and companies that rank high, are perceived to be highly-credible, because they perform at the top of Google's analysis of quality content.

As a result, many of our clients invest significantly in 'content-properties', as soon as they understand the logic, and witness the strategy's proven results. Those that take that approach, increase website 'hits' and 'unique views' within months of their launch. Rest assured Danny, I expect we will have the same results with your business."

Glancing up, and noticing the quickly-approaching darkness of the nighttime-sky, Josh added: "I know that was likely a lot of new information for you tonight. There is much more to share, but is there anything I mentioned tonight that was not comprehendible, if not fully understandable?"

"It is a lot to take-in, all at once", I admitted. "But it was logical and clear to me, that we have significant online opportunity, to multiply our qualified 'claims' prospects. And produce more profit from our revenue", I added. "Thanks for staying out here tonight a little longer than I know you had planned".

"My pleasure, Danny", said Josh; both of us, already making our way toward the edge of the dock-side 'guest' slip.

Turning the key, Josh's Sea-Ray sprung to life; with a low-level, but powerful growl. The bow-line in my hand, Josh gave me an 'ok' nod, to secure it to the starboard-side cleat. As the 'Sundancer' began to slowly reverse away from the dock, into the darkness; he added:

"See you tomorrow, Danny."

Key Takeaways - Chapter 5

'Paid Advertising versus Organic Ranking'

When I use Adwords to promote my business, and 'rent' from Google: they are my landlord. Or, I can build 'content-properties' over time, and build equity – like investing in my own home.

'High-Ranking Organic Content'

To build high-ranking 'content-properties', I need to learn and develop:

An understanding of the criteria that Google uses to 'rank' their organic search-results

An understanding of the 'Subject Categories' (SC's) most relevant to my target prospects

An ability to create SC content that is unique and educational to the person searching, *and* is effective at 'ranking' high

'Continuous-Improvement'

From the first day we opened the firm, I envisioned building effective 'systems' for processing and administration. That I could do the same with 'marketing', was eye-opening. For me, the most impactful statement from Josh was Peter Drucker's quote: ***What gets measured, gets managed.***

'Attribution and Evidence-Based Marketing'

I did not realize that online and offline data could be consolidated and analyzed, to make better sales and marketing decisions, using 'data-analytics'. And I could understand why Josh put emphasis on the importance of 'attribution': of our being able to specifically correlate, which of our marketing activities are most effective, and profitable.

If, like me, you can see the value in what I learned that day with Josh; take a moment to reflect on each of the above points, in relation to your business, and its growth potential.

When deployed in your business, what might the applications, and results, look like for your company?

CHAPTER 6
The Lake: Part 3
('Review Marketing')

There is something about the fresh-air of cottage-country, that has always provided me a deep, sound sleep. As a young adult, I was fortunate to have friends with summer homes, on both sides of the border. What I remember most, is waterskiing by day, and bonfires by night. And the blackness, that surrounded the light from the fire.

I think it was the consistent, rhythmic chorus of waves washing ashore, that helped me to sleep so well back then; and on that first night at Lake Rosseau. Those long-gone youthful days, were near-free of responsibility: beyond school, and earning my way through college. Thinking back, that same relaxed feeling was beginning to take-root again: after hearing, understanding, and seeing a path through our previously-considered, insurmountable business challenges.

That first day spent with Josh, was as much empowering, as it was calming. I had found an experienced guide, that would surely help Melissa and I push through – what was to that point – the most difficult period we faced as a couple, as individuals, and what I had ever experienced in my career. No matter how difficult the ensuing months back in Orchard

Park would undoubtedly be, I was becoming more confident that we would persevere, as would 'the firm'.

Melissa arose shortly after me, around 6:00am. We started the day, with coffee on the front porch, barely fifteen-minutes since the sun arose over the eastern shore. The lake was as still as glass; a fine-mist hovered just above the water's surface; and we could hear the echo of loon-calls, coming from what sounded like, just beyond the southern edge of our narrow, limited view of the lake. I shared with Melissa, an overview of my Friday discussions with Josh, to bring her up-to-speed; though mostly, to let her know that I expected our current cost-cutting action-plan, would likely get some relief in the coming months, with a boost to the firm's revenue. Though, I was cautiously optimistic about the timeline, to keep us both grounded, and focussed. I could tell by her expression and relaxed posture, that the combination of good news, and the peaceful weekend surroundings, were just what she needed too. She was pleased to hear that Josh planned to continue our discussion, around mid-afternoon – after our return from a late-morning cruise with Pete and Robyn, through the Port Carling Lock, to nearby Lake Muskoka.

...

Turning to his left from the 'captain's chair', Pete strained his vocal chords, to overcome a combination of the engine's-snarl and the swirling-wind that whooshed over the windscreen of his Maxum 2600 Cruiser – while carving its' way through the moderate-chop of Lake Muskoka.

"There's 'Lady Muskoka', Danny. Massive, isn't she!?", he prompted; while pointing to the now-visible, three-level, one-hundred-and-four-foot-long, freshwater, day-cruise ship – that carried about 300 passengers, around the Muskoka region; for mid-afternoon tours. As we approached from a safe distance, to her port-side, I could see a number of vertical spray-streams and rooster tails, created by a group of small-craft, that criss-crossed her four-foot-plus, trailing wake and swell. A half dozen or so, jet skies and small, 12-foot aluminium, outboard motor-boats, sailed through the air, as they jumped the waves: resembling a bunch of skateboarders, who had just found the best 'launch ramp' in town.

As we slowed down to get a closer look at the ship, I asked: "Did you ever try that, Pete?", pointing to the young, daredevil-boaters, we could now hear: hooping and hollering their exuberance, and cheering one-another – the more air separating a boat from the water, the higher their volume and enthusiasm.

"Not me... but my son Kel, and his local friends started that tradition about twenty years ago". I found out about the stunt one-weekend, when his pal Stephen, cut too-close to the 'grand lady's' wake: launching his tiny 10-foot, aluminium fishing-boat completely out of the water, while simultaneously catching a head-on gust of wind that lifted the bow vertical, and back-flipped the boat. Fortunately, he was thrown a few-feet out of the falling craft's path. He wasn't seriously hurt, but that put an end to those stunts for a number of years, once the news travelled around the region", Pete recalled: with a fond, reflective look on his face.

"How is Kel these days, Pete? I don't recall meeting him", I asked.

"He's doing very well, thanks. He discovered fairly early-on, that he's a natural for real-estate and stock investment… and turned that into his full-time occupation, over the years. I am very proud of who he has become: a loving father, a great listener, and he has a sharp wit, to match his keen mind. We laugh a lot, when we hang-out together; though regrettably, we were too busy over the years, to see each other as much as I would have preferred. But we're both doing a better job with that now. Time passes so quickly, Danny. Keep that top of mind, with Melissa and your family. All the rest of it is 'window-dressing'. And it's easy to get caught-up in the 'distractions'; that in the end, don't have much *real* meaning, when you look back".

"Does Kel come up to the cottage much?", I asked.

With a warm, pleased smile, he said: "actually, next weekend, he and his wife Sandra, are bringing my grandson Jeremy, up for a few days."

I acknowledged, with a nod, before briefly drifting to thoughts of doing the same some-day, with Melissa and a family of our own.

We cruised back to Lake Rosseau, shortly thereafter, and anchored about a hundred yards off of Tobin Island; safely out of the 'busy-boating-lanes'. After a quiet lunch on-board, it was time to head back to the cottage. We docked, and secured the Maxum in the boathouse around 2 o'clock: leaving about an hour for us to 'kick-back', before Josh's expected arrival.

About twenty-minutes-to-three, I offered to go down to the dock, to help Josh with the boat; while Pete prepared his special, steak-marinade, for that night's supper; and Robyn took Melissa for an off-property walk, through a partially-trodden nature trail, that the Samson clan had carved-out over the years.

Gurgling into its 'slip' for the day, Josh skillfully navigated the Sundancer into position, while I caught the pulpit; before leaning-in to grab, and tie-off, the bow-line. We made our way up to the cottage, and joined in the dinner prep-work with Pete; true to our double-duty dinner agreement, with Melissa and Robyn. With the 'surf-and-turf' now marinating in the fridge, we had at least 90-mintues to stretch on the porch, before firing-up the king-sized Webber grill, that we had cleverly-planned to fulfill our cooking of the entire evening's menu.

"Danny, has our resident online-guru had anything useful to

share with you, so far?", Pete opened the conversation, with a friendly half-jab at our mutual marketing-mentor; knowing full-well, that Josh more-than filled the role. Before I could utter a word, Josh broke-in, insisting that he was less than worthy of wearing that title, or anything close to it.

"Pete loves to get me going, Danny. And some times, it actually works", he began: with a friendly nod toward his dear-friend, before continuing on: "there is very little that I actually know, Danny; and anything that I have learned, has been generously shared with me by people like this old-lug here", he added, while playfully glancing in Pete's direction. "I am not a smart man. If I had to take an IQ test, my guess is, I would fall smack-dab in the mid-average category: if that! Problem-solving is not my strong-suit; nor is creativity, process development, or analytical thinking. Unlike Pete's brilliant legal mind; my wife Olena's keen design-thinking brain, or Melissa's natural knack for numbers, I am merely a business generalist; that has had the good-fortune of being exposed to so-many exceptionally sharp-minds over the decades; and had just enough good-sense to ask questions, and absorb as much as I could, from all of them. The truth is, while I have been somewhat branded as an online marketer, my team behind the scenes are the brilliant ones, that deserve the vast majority of the credit, for all that we have accomplished together. If I am above average in anything, it is the ability to find and choose people much-smarter than me, to work with; to stay out of their way, and facilitate, as best I can, the application of their highly-developed skills to their fullest potential. I realize that probably sounds cliché, but it has been my secret of success, since the day I was forced to sell my first business, many years ago".

"See, I told ya Danny; Josh won't take credit for the business sage that he is", Pete threw-in, with a cackle-laugh, that likely had its origins from the early trailer-park days, in Kentucky. "You're a good man Josh, for putting up with me over the years", he added; before raising his just-filled beer-mug, and toasting the humble nature of his closest friend. "To Josh… and his newest protégé, Danny. Cheers gentleman!"

"Cheers!" Our three mugs clanked in-sync, along with the jovial tribute; followed by the satisfied-sound of three frothy, ice-cold, 'Canadians', being gratefully consumed.

A few moments later, Josh broke the silence: "Pete, do you mind if we continue our discussion about Danny's company, until supper?"

"Absolutely, Josh, please… go ahead", Pete replied.

"Thanks Pete", Josh acknowledged; and continued: "yesterday, we spent some time talking about the use of 'content-properties', to raise 'organic'-search-ranking, and drive more qualified-leads to the firm. Let's continue now, moving-on to a very important component to the process of converting prospects into customers: 'Review Marketing'. To understand its relevance, we need to back-track somewhat, to our earlier discussion about websites, and the components of an effective 'website path' – that leads a viewer toward the 'action' you want them to take. As you likely recall, the most notable of Aristotle's persuasion principles is Ethos: the instilling of trust and credibility, to enhance and support, the integrity of the character/author/organization that is presenting the case for making a purchase of your company's product or service. It is important to provide evidence of the business' trustworthiness early, within the visitor's experience on your website; so that they can mentally 'check' *trust,* off of their list. While you can tell the reader all the reason's that they should listen and believe you, the most powerful method of instilling trust, is developed from the reference point of third parties: those that do not have a vested interest in either side of the transaction, being considered. While the notion of reviews, testimonials, and referrals is not new, the internet facilitates past and current evaluations of companies through a multitude of formats and locations today, such as Google Reviews, aggregated review websites like Yelp and Trip Advisor, in addition to customer comments and experiences shared on social media channels: such as Twitter, Facebook, and LinkedIn. While these public evaluations of your company's service carry some benefit, there are three distinct disadvantages to consider – for equally important reasons:

1. Unless consistently monitored, negative and fake "reviews" may be left unaddressed and will spread

(people are 2.5x more likely to share a negative review than a positive review)

2. Many of these websites display paid, competitor advertising *on your review page*

3. The 'ranking' benefit of online reviews (user generated content) is attributed to *their* website, <u>not yours</u>

Most smaller businesses, believe it is effective to simply reproduce on their website, reviews that have been posted on other third-party sites; we call that 'duplicate content'. 'Lady Muskoka' the cruise ship you saw today, is an ideal example of that mistake. Their website contains a great deal of 'duplicate content', which can actually *penalize* your organic ranking. In addition, a prospect seeing 'Trip Advisor' all over the website, may choose to go *there*, to look at alternative cruise-ships for comparison; rather than stay on the site, and buy tickets. The marketers at "Lady Muskoka' appreciate the value of online reviews, they are just falling a little short on execution.

To give online reviews some context, if you don't mind, I would like to share some statistics with you?", Josh asked.

"Sure", I confirmed.

"Thanks, Danny. These are the reasons my companies, and our clients, are all invested in 'review marketing':

72% of consumers will **take action** online after reading a positive review

88% of online shoppers **incorporate reviews** into the purchase decision process

Products with **reviews sell over 200% more** than products that have no reviews or ratings

88% of people read reviews *to determine the quality* of a local business

42% of e-commerce sites **report an increase** in average order value *after* including reviews of products

"What do you think, Danny?", Josh asked.

"Taking what you've shared with me so far, about marketing 'the firm' online, 'review marketing' makes sense. it's logical. But other than monitoring, and prompting customers to submit reviews to Google, I don't yet see what *we can do* to better utilize reviews?', I queried.

"I understand. That is the perspective that most business owners have. Let's think outside-the-box for a moment. How can we overcome those three disadvantages of third-party review platforms, that I mentioned earlier: remember, what they were?"

"I can't remember verbatim, but I understood them as: *lack of control* to address negative, and intentionally harmful online evaluations; reviews of my service can be used by those third-party platforms, to **sell or re-direct readers to my competitor's services** or products; and the third was… ah, yes: online reviews of my service are considered **valuable 'user generated content', or 'ranking-juice'**, that only benefit the platform or website that they are initially posted-on", I answered.

"Perfect. So, in an ideal world, what situation would solve all three of these negative effects, or missed opportunities for the firm?", Josh continued.

"Well, I don't have the time or resources to do this, but you said think outside the box… I guess we could start our own review site for legal services?"

"You are close, Danny. That solution might also benefit your competition, and I think it may be a tough-sell, to get your competitors to encourage *their* customers to post on a site that you own. Keep going…", he prompted.

"'Can we adapt a review function into *our* existing website?", I offered.

"Absolutely", Josh immediately replied; and added a grin, before continuing. "When a prospect is considering your firm's service, they will more often than not, Google search: the 'name of your company' along with the word 'review' or reviews'. Your own review platform, can be indexed in such a way, that it ranks highly within organic search returns, and a click-through will re-direct prospects to that page on your site, rather than elsewhere. It will also empower you to address negative reviews in a timely manner, and block from search-engine access, any intentionally harmful evaluations, left by non-customers. You acquire valuable 'user generated content' to boost 'ranking' authority, and can be confident that prospects will not be exposed to competitive solicitations. Make sense, Danny?", he asked.

"Completely. What about motivating customers to post reviews… how have your other clients been successful with that challenge?", I probed.

"Satisfied clients are generally agreeable to posting a positive review. The challenge is that the task gets lost in the shuffle of their busy lives. It is all about timing… and especially about how you ask, and how often. What I suggest to clients, is that the request for a review is introduced in the late stages of the sales cycle; as a near-condition of doing business. You will have brought to their attention by that point the company's positive and rectified moderate reviews, and simply ask them that if they were to purchase your service, and had a favourable experience, is there any reason that they would not be comfortable providing a review of the service. As part of the close, after there is agreement, there is a subtle reminder – and some include the commitment to making a review in the agreement. If the company is doing their job properly while delivering the service, there is an intermittent 'check-in' to discover their informal evaluation of the service. Once the transaction has been fulfilled, the review is provided. Granted, with this process you will not receive 100% compliance, but it will be well-above 50% if you do the job right… and those reviews, as you have already seen, are worth future revenue.

"What questions do you have so far, Danny?", Josh asked.

"Ah…, just one. When can we get started…?"

Key Takeaways - Chapter 6

'Why Use Review Marketing?'

I don't know about you, but these statistics were more than enough to convince me of the value of 'Review Marketing':

72% of consumers will **take action** online after reading a positive review

88% of online shoppers **incorporate reviews** into the purchase decision process

Products with **reviews sell over 200% more** than products that have no reviews or ratings

88% of people read reviews *to determine the quality* of a local business

42% of e-commerce sites **report an increase** in average order value *after* including reviews of products

'Third-Party' versus 'Your Own Review Platform'

The disadvantages of relying upon 3rd party websites, to house your online reviews:

1. Unless consistently monitored, negative and fake "reviews" may be left unaddressed and will spread (people are 2.5x more likely to share a negative review than a positive review)

2. Many 3rd Party 'Review' websites display paid, competitor advertising *on your review page*

3. The 'ranking' benefit of online reviews (user generated content) is attributed to *their* website, not yours

'How to get More Reviews from Customers'

Satisfied clients are generally agreeable to posting a positive review. It is all about timing… and especially about how you ask,

Pro Tips:

- Introduce the anticipated request for a review, within the sales cycle.

- Add a subtle reminder, as part of the close, after there is agreement.

- 'Check-in' during the service, by asking the client: if you were to rate us today, what might it be?

- Once the transaction has been fulfilled, the review should be requested

CHAPTER 7
The Commitment
('Facebook Marketing')

There have been three occasions in my life, when I knew *exactly* what I wanted.

It was that way with my interest in the law. I recall, at a very-young age, watching my father Robert, working after supper in the spare-bedroom – that was converted into a small office: case files strewn on an old, rustic wooden wedding-table, that doubled as his desk. It looked to me like important work. The dinner-time conversations with my mother Lorraine, about his case-load as a young 'public defender', would occasionally become heated. Her dual role of caregiver *and* career-bound consultant, and *his* demanding schedule at 'the County' – combined with long, night-time and weekend hours in the home-office – took its toll on both of them. I suspect that was the driving force behind their divorcing, when I was twelve. Nonetheless, by the time I started high school, I had decided the law was for me, and was committed to becoming an attorney, no matter how long it took, or how much sweat and sacrifice was needed to get there.

Similarly, the day I met Melissa at the UB Quad, we instantly connected as friends, and it was obvious to both of us, that there was attraction. It was a difficult period – juggling the completion of an Environmental LL.M. degree, and interviewing with local and out of town law firms, while Melissa was adapting to life as a second-year undergraduate student. The relationship was slow to start, but I knew what I wanted, and made the commitment to figure-out how to be an ambitious professional, *and* an engaged life-partner – determined not to make the same mistakes, my folks did.

Starting 'The Davidson Firm', was no different. Though admittedly, before the weekend at Lake Rosseau, there were times when subtle, second-thoughts, would creep-in: usually, in the wee hours of the morning, when everything was quiet and still. I was left alone with thoughts of uncertainty: did I have the business skills to build our tiny firm into the success story, I knew was possible? For me, that weekend was somewhat like hitting 'refresh' on the browser, while on a website – the vast majority of what is visible on the screen remains the same; though, if you look closely, you often 'see' aspects of content, you missed the first time 'round. What became clear to me over the course of that pivotal weekend, was that the commitment I had made to build 'the firm', was never *really* in-question.

While it *was* only a week ago, our Sunday discussion (centered around Facebook marketing) brought it all home, for me. I recognized that – more than being an encyclopedia of tactics and strategy – Josh displayed an uncanny ability to explain things with simplicity; adding context to make his points easily digestible. Gaining a clearer understanding of the 'big picture' of how a business *functions and prospers*, had been the most significant shift he provided me. As Melissa and I sat on our front-porch, I did my best to 'debrief' her, about what I had learned from Josh over those three days. She was keen on Facebook advertising early-on, so I saved that till last...

"It sounds like you are leaning towards reallocating what we spend on Facebook, to 'content-properties' and 'review marketing'", Melissa asked; with a hint of questioning-doubt in her tone. She picked up the concepts quickly, and was already thinking ahead, like the 'quant' that she is.

"The jury is still out on that, Mel. I have started to work with Josh and his team, to discover what our mix of marketing investment should look like, based on the 'return on investment' of our current marketing activities. Regardless of the mix, we'll use all three of the lead-generating tools. Josh reminded me, that our current marketing campaigns do not necessarily represent the potential effectiveness of each of those marketing platforms, so we will do some A/B testing with new 'creative', that Josh's team is working on, with me.

"That makes sense", she replied; then, added: "did you learn anything new about Facebook-marketing'"

"Good question. Let me see what I can recall, on the spot...

Like Google Adwords, Facebook is a powerful marketing tool; and neither one is 'better' than the other. A smart marketing mix utilizes their lead-generation tools in concert with each other; and incorporates 'learning' from one – into the campaign decisions and improvements of the other. For our particular business, we are looking for the most cost-effective way to find individuals who qualify for compensation claims.

The 'lowest hanging fruit' in our case, are claimants that have applied on their own – and been 'denied' on their first application. The reason is, those folks will be looking for assistance in the appeal process. They have already identified their 'problem' and realize that they cannot solve it on their own. With these particular prospects, they will look to a search engine, most likely Google, to find expert help. Our 'content-property' strategy is being developed around the Subject Category of "claims appeal attorney'. Josh is doing keyword-search research and testing, for us to identify the content and ads that will serve as bait, to 'hook' these prospects online. While we build and expand content – rather than fishing with a few 'poles' in the vast ocean, that is the internet – we will be casting an ever-wider, yet dense, 'net', of sorts, around each Subject Category that we identify. Another Subject Category we are developing is for qualified 'first-time' claimants, that are already aware of compensation programs, but not comfortable going through the process on their own. Josh expects three Subject Categories will be an ideal starting point for our content-property strategy."

"That makes sense Danny, but what about Facebook?", Melissa asked.

"Josh defined the difference in strategy, something like this: Facebook is a platform where we can find new customers, by helping them to identify that they do, in fact, qualify for compensation. On the other hand, Google is the platform we use to help new customers find us". In other words, Google is more effective for 'hooking' those prospects who already know that they have a problem, and are searching for a solution – they need help navigating the administration process of a 'claim' or appeal... now.

However, with Facebook's social marketing platform, we start with a prospect profile of 'traits' (or demographics) that a likely claimant may have: they live within a 30-mile radius of a facility that previous claimants worked at; they are between 55 and 80 years old; they are below the median income level in their region, and so on. Our messaging will be focussed on helping the target reader to identify that *they may* be eligible for a claim; however, a target reader/viewer that falls within the same 'demographic group' or profile, does not necessarily mean they were ever harmed or made ill at work.

As a result, we use a very different communication strategy for each of the platforms, and content-properties".

"Does that make sense", I asked.

"Yes. And it sounds to me, that Google would generate more qualified leads than Facebook", she replied.

"That would be right, if both ad platforms had an equal cost per click-through. And bare in mind that we're working within a tight marketing budget. Google Adwords average cost-per-click is about double, that of Facebook; depending upon which source you read. And that's just an average. In the legal industry, for example, some keyword strings can be bid-up to several hundred dollars per click. As Josh explained though, those cost comparisons are not relevant. The most important metric to focus on is profitability. Josh's team is working on that analysis for us, and as we run future campaigns on both platforms, we will be able to optimize every ad dollar we spend; investing it where it returns the most money to our bank account".

"So, once we know which platform generates the most prospects, and closed business, why would we not put all our eggs in that basket?", she astutely asked.

"Are you gunning for my job, Mel?", I playfully asked.

"Ha-ha, no thanks", she half-laugh replied; adding "I'm not the one who wanted to build a company, Danny", she said with an implied grin. "Being 'President' is all yours, honey. I'm just focussed on how we can grow the business, and build security into our family's future", she added: revealing the concern of our current financial situation.

"I hear ya, Mel. It is going to appear to get harder, before it gets better. Let me answer your question, based on what Josh shared with me, and what we somewhat already know, and agree on. For the firm to be successful over the long-term, and survive the short-term challenges, we need to manage a delicate balance between short-term optimization, and building long-term systems. You're right, in that, when the numbers come back next week, we'll steer our marketing investment towards the platform that produces higher short-term results. But look at it like you would traditional financial investment. You would not place all of your portfolio into one category: like bonds, stocks, or savings; nor would you invest within one of those categories in one bond issue, one stock, or one savings-vehicle; because conditions are always changing.

We will invest in 'content-property', because that is the firm's future nest-egg. We will invest in 'review' marketing, because it boosts the effectiveness of the other three: Google ads, Facebook ads, and Content-Properties. What we don't yet know, is *which* ad platform outperforms the other, related to the specific ads that we run for the service. The analysis work that Josh's team is doing for us, includes a data-driven system that allows us to consistently monitor the profitability of all of our activities over time. That will be our ongoing 'reality check' of what is working, and what is changing within the business. More importantly, we will be able to correlate why those changes are occurring, and how to adapt our decisions and actions."

"It sounds like Josh has been quite an influence on you, Danny. You sound like the President of a company, and less like an attorney. It's a little strange. I wasn't expecting that, but I should have known that all of this learning would change you, over time", she reflected.

"Really? I suppose, I do feel somewhat different. How have I changed?", I probed.

"It's a good thing, honey. You're still the same person that I married. Maybe change is the wrong description of what I've been noticing. I think it's more-so a return of two traits that I had known you always to have", she said.

"Really... what are they?", I asked.

"Confident and committed...", she said, smiling her response.

Key Takeaways - Chapter 7

'Facebook Ads versus Google Adwords'

I appreciated how Josh differentiated Google and Facebook platforms, in terms of prospect types:

Facebook is a platform where <u>we can find new customers</u>, by *helping them to identify* that they do, in fact, have a need for our service (our product). Facebook is also effective for 'switching' loyalty – of products or services that are sold by competitors, and consumed on a regular basis.

Google is the platform we use to help <u>new customers find us</u>": *those who already know* that they have a problem, and are searching for a solution.

Pro Tips:

1. For your primary product or service, take a moment to consider both platforms, in relation to the 'need awareness' level of your prospects.

2. Define which 'Subject Category'(SC) is most relevant to prospects that are 'searching for a solution' like yours. Which SC would be most relevant to a prospect you are attempting to 'switch' from a competitor?

'Digital Marketing Mix'

Three steps to measuring digital marketing profitability:

1. Determine 'The Lifetime Value of a Customer' (LTV)

2. Run an online marketing campaign on Facebook and Google, and trace which 'online source' generated each new customer.

3. Using your LTV, calculate the profitability of your Google Adwords and Facebook Ads campaigns.

Bear in mind, that your initial Ad campaigns are not necessarily a gauge of Facebook or Google's advertising potential. A/B testing on both platforms should improve your response rate, and help you to further refine ad content within your key 'Subject Categories'.

CHAPTER 8
'Putting It All Together'

July and August in Western New York can be humid and scorching hot. The Summer of 2012 was particularly extreme; appropriately matching the pace of our growth, relative to the previous quarter. I went 'all-in' with the claims-side of our business; and spent none of my precious-time on business development for new litigation clients. By the end of September, revenue from approved claims was up by 31% over Q2, and we fully expected to exceed that performance in the last quarter of 2012. That confidence came from the upward trajectory of our online metrics; most notably, were 'visits' and 'average time' spent on the website. On their own, these indicators would not influence my optimism all that much, but when correlated with a similar rise in our 'enquiry-to-closed-claims' ratio, I knew that we were on the right path.

Back in early June, I worked with Josh and his team to re-structure the website, in-line with Aristotle's persuasion principles. It was hard work, but well worth it. Josh kept pushing me deeper into the understanding of our customers, so that we could more-effectively communicate with future prospects. I spent hours on the phone with past clients; both successful and unsuccessful claimants, to absorb as much as they would share with me, such as: their expectations before engaging our service, why they chose our service over another, how they found us, and would they recommend us to others; among many other 'call-objectives' that Josh armed me with, beforehand. If they were pleased with our service, I shared my appreciation if they would kindly provide their evaluation of our service, on our very own, newly-launched 'review platform'.

Within sixty-days, we had the platform populated with over 50 positive reviews from the previous year's client list. Some of our past customers were shocked, when I encouraged them to post an honest review of their experience, even if they were voicing a disappointed opinion. Those customers were few and far between, but 90% of the negative sentiment I heard, was based upon an expectation that they had, that did not clearly reflect reality. In all likelihood, our communication may not have been clear enough from the outset. That discovery was worth its weight in gold! I listened a lot, and shared what happened with their case in detail. A few posted their rating and story on the platform. I promptly acknowledged and addressed their review online, as Josh had encouraged me to do. He advised that in his experience, website visitors will not believe your reviews if they are 100% positive, 5-star ratings. I remember Josh's words so clearly, he said: "remember Ethos, Danny. Believability and trust are dependent on honesty and integrity. No person, and no business is perfect. By hearing the authentic reporting of a dissatisfied, but acknowledged and rectified customer, your credibility and trustworthiness will go through the roof, in the eyes of your prospects. Just as important, those readers that become customers, will not adopt a similar, unrealistic expectation.

Most encouraging, was the latter half of June, and the month of July. Our content-properties were still in-development, yet our enquiries were on the rise. Josh walked me through the website's analytics, and it was clear that in the past, with our 'old' website, we were missing opportunities. The site was previously not converting visits into enquires at an impressive ratio. While I was eager to boost our Adwords campaign budget immediately after the analysis indicated it was more profitable (for us) than Facebook, he strongly encouraged me to hold-off until the website was turned into an effective 'stream-lined-path'; that would convert more visits into enquiries. "We are only paying for 'visits'", he said. "Why waste money on visits, when what we are interested-in is qualified enquiries: enquiries that can be turned into claims, that can be turned into cash". Let's finish the website, and then increase the Adwords budget, while we build-out your portfolio of 'content-properties", he logically explained.

As usual, Josh was right.

To keep costs down, we kept Cassy to 2 ½ days per week, while Melissa and I continued to carry the balance of the claims processing work. I was beginning to take note of Cassy's near-weekly comments about needing more hours, and was concerned that she may leave us, if she found more work elsewhere. Hearing this, Josh had an analysis performed, on the various types of medical-based claims that we processed on behalf of customers, and we learned some unexpected, useful gems, that impacted the efficiency and profitability of the firm, beyond simply administrative processing.

Beforehand, we had a few conference-call discussions with Josh and his team, and agreed that there was significant value to the business, in being able to answer three important questions:

1. How can we reduce the time and cost to process a claim?

2. Which customers are the most profitable, and how can we identify them?

3. How can we attract more of our 'best' customers?

Turns out, that this examination had far reaching implications for our short-term cash flow challenges, and long-term growth and profitability opportunities of the firm. Josh uncovered the fact that 68% of our claims submitted to the Government were approved on the first submission. And just over forty-percent *of those,* were processed, approved, and paid-out within 58 days; which is amazing, given the overall average time from 'enquiry to pay out' was 97 days! Recognizing that cash-flow was a short-term, high priority for us, he identified the traits of those claims and claimants, so that we could more-tightly focus our paid ad campaign messaging – to entice a higher proportion of *those customers* to click-through our ads, and fill-out a 'free claim-evaluation' form on the landing page.

It worked!

Internally, we labelled that target segment as "Quick-Claims', because the research and processing time turned out to be about 31% less than our average. The data suggested that the 'simplicity' of those claim-types indicated faster processing by government administrators, and a higher approval rate. Our 'payout-fee' for 'quick-claims' was in the bottom third of revenue, but I could easily see that with some further automation, and process streamlining, we could reduce our labor cost and timeline. Boosting their profit, 'Quick-claims' had the potential to be a cash-cow, that Josh and I both felt, was the key to weathering the next four to six months, while further ramping-up the 'marketing machine'.

At the other end of the spectrum, were our largest revenue-generating customers. These were more- complicated medical cases, involving claimants whose illnesses were much harder to prove causation, from their job. Many took as long as a year, and rarely, a few extended beyond that. But our 'payout-fee' was around ***four-times*** that of 'quick-claims', and they were just over ***forty-percent more profitable***, when we included all related costs. We internally branded those claims as 'Long-shots'. Josh went to work on 'content-properties' for the 'Long-shot' segment, knowing that a large, growing stable of those customers would be the heart of the business, long-term.

There was still a lot to learn about our customers, and even more that we could automate, in the process. As Josh explained in our November conference call, while the firm has some sound 'procedures' in place, we should combine 'analysis' with 'automation' plans. In other words, automation should serve the dual-purpose of reducing expenses, *and* gathering of intelligence about our customers, or process performance. He said: "...going back to Deming's 'continuous improvement' principles; remember Danny, that the goal is to constantly learn and improve every aspect of the business, through measurement. What we learn in the 'operational' side of the business, has benefits to online marketing, customer-care, and accounting; and vice-versa. It is all interconnected, just like any other eco-system.

The other benefit of having automated, and documented systems, is that the 'learning' that occurs, within the brains of your staff, does not disappear, if and when they leave. More importantly, your plans to expand and scale the claims business, are dependent on your commitment to capturing and using information, and knowledge. From what you have told me so far, I would give Cassy six-months, at best, before she leaves. She is competent, and looking for other opportunities. It is important that you make it a priority to document your processes soon. Is that something Melissa could work on with Cassy?", he said, in a combination advisory-asking tone".

"I think so. They have a good relationship. Cassy will pick-up on the fact that we are somewhat preparing for her departure, but Melissa can manage that just fine. Cassy and Melissa have a good relationship; at least, it is closer than the one she and I have. I will talk to Melissa, and put that in motion", I replied.

By early December, Melissa had documented, step-by-step, the most efficient claims administration process, based on a collective-understanding she gained from examining how each of the three of us, recorded, researched, and prepared claim-submissions to the Government. There were still improvements to be made, but Josh acknowledged that her documentation was good-enough for us to use to automate much more of the process. We agreed to license, and pay for some modifications of proprietary software that Josh's company had developed.

At the beginning of Q2 2013, the firm was back to break-even, in spite of our concluding relationships with two, of our remaining four, corporate clients. We increased our marketing budget by 30% over the last six months, so, when we reported break-even, it was somewhat misleading of our progress. We were growing consistently, and re-investing aggressively into the business. We started with thirty 'content-properties', and projected we would own over one-hundred, by the end of 2013. They were 'paying for themselves', from the volume of qualified leads they generated, and then some. Our 'enquiry-to-closed-claims' ratio was growing. Josh and his team continued to manage and optimize our Google Adwords and Facebook marketing campaigns; and as a collective, we monitored our newly-created 'dashboard' of key metrics; and tweaked, changed, tested, and re-tested all aspects of our marketing, systematically.

We projected, based on our current trajectory of learning and increased growth, that we could double the business year-over-year, by the end of 2013. It was an aggressive goal.

August of 2013 was… well, it was the month from hell. We contracted a small HR company to help us hire our second employee. Cassy was back to full-time, and the whining about hours had subsided, only to be replaced by her not-so-subtle demands for more money. Under normal circumstances, I would have been comfortable paying her more, and was planning to give her a healthy raise at the end of the year, when I would have a better handle on the consistency of our improving financial position. She was also growing a little 'too big for her britches'. I think she was beginning to associate her now 'at-capacity' work volume with being taken advantage of. I wasn't sure if it was due in-part to her getting engaged, to long-time boyfriend Sergei, or if it was something else. Nonetheless, I realized that an HR professional would work with us to develop accountabilities and objectives, in addition to creating a 'profile' of future candidates to be incorporated into our anticipated, growing workforce.

Holly Newstead was a one-woman-show: a career HR professional with a diversity of experience, depth of skills, and a jovial personality that made her easy to work with. Human Resources was never Melissa nor my strong suit. What we didn't know at the time, was that Cassy and Sergei were planning, behind the scenes, to expand his small legal practise into our domain: compensation claims!

I was livid, at first. It was a Tuesday… the sixteenth, I believe; when Josh called me to break the news. His team was doing some online research, and testing of various keywords, when they discovered a local-listing that caught their attention: a Google Ad for Sergei Barenov LLP, offering our exact service.

Competition is healthy. I am a strong supporter of free markets, and believe that everyone has the right to open any business, in any category – including mine. But it was the 'sting' of betrayal, that annoyed me beyond normal levels of composure; when Josh's self-initiated investigation, uncovered that Cassy had attempted to copy and extract a version of his proprietary software, that we had licensed, and customized for claims-processing.

Rather than approach Cassy, I called Holly in, to discuss what my options were, and sent Pete an email, to get his take on a course of action. I suspected that if we spent some time digging deeper, we would find more ammunition to support an immediate termination. But in New York State, we have to sometimes err on the side of caution, when it comes to employees. Especially an employee that is engaged to an attorney, and one that it appeared, was attempting to hijack my business. As far as I know, Sergei was 'small-time': providing notary-public services, representing small-claims disputes, and property management services on behalf of landlords attempting to evict tenants. Had I known she was seeing Sergei before I hired her, I would have thought twice about the decision.

Holly initially suggested we take a strong stance, to see how Cassy reacted. Our preference was that she resign, and I would pay out a generous six-weeks severance – given the situation – to avoid a messy, legal dispute that would surely distract us from the far more important tasks that we needed to focus on.

Pete generously agreed to discuss the situation the next day, via phone, with Holly in my office. His first words, when asked his general opinion was: "well Danny, in my experience, where there's smoke, there's fire. It is likely, that Josh's 'servers' will uncover further evidence, if she has attempted to acquire any other information from your system". (I thought to myself, thank goodness we agreed to host all of our software and email accounts on his server. And that Josh insisted on each of us signing an access and disclosure document, was a godsend).

We decided to have Josh look at the meta-data of her company email account, to see if there was anything suspicious that warranted a deeper look. The most significant concern, was that we had upwards of $150k in longer-term claims in various stages of processing. While Cassy would have been risking a lot to steal client records, Sergei, by association, would have been making an even bigger mistake. I did not know him that well, but what I did know, I had little respect for.

Time was of the essence. It was decided we would ask Josh, to see what could be uncovered by 3pm the following day, and we would confront her at 4:30.

The next day, with the three of us sitting around the circular table in our small conference room, we had Pete introduce himself, via speaker phone, as counsel for the firm. Holly then proceeded to place in front of Cassy, a host of incriminating documentation, that clearly caught her off-guard, based on the immediate 'droop' in her facial expression, from 'pleasant' to 'worry'. There was no discussion, or questions asked of Cassy; rather, I presented our generous severance offer to her in writing, and allowed Pete to walk her through the conditions – which included an immediate withdrawal of the offer, if she chose not to sign the agreement on the spot; a 'mutual release' of further action from both parties; and a confidentiality clause.

I made one, short statement, while extending a pen, and looking her straight in the eyes. In a half-warning, half-questioning tone, I said: "it's a small town we live in… *isn't it, Cassy?*"

She held my gaze for a brief second-or-so, before her head slowly bowed-down, toward the table, in shame. After a deep sigh, she picked up the pen, and signed the agreement.

With the traitor in our midst, now removed, I was determined not to let this setback effect the company's momentum. Holly returned to the conference room – having escorted our former employee out of the building, along with her personal belongings.

Seated across from me at the table, with a pen at the ready, and her lined note pad, flipped-open to a fresh page; she began: "alright, let's get started on finding you a 'claims-processing' replacement".

Maybe it was my reaction to the betrayal. Or perhaps it was my 'driven' personality-trait taking over… I really don't know where the next words came from. But without hesitation, or any semblance of thought, I simply responded: "better make it *three*, Holly…"

Key Takeaways - Chapter 8

'Most Profitable Customers'

If you can answer these 3 questions thoroughly and accurately, your business will grow, when the answers are put into action:

1. How can we reduce the time and cost to process a product or deliver a service?

2. Which of our customers are the most profitable, and how can we identify them?

3. How can we attract more of our 'best', most profitable customers?

Pro Tip:

- When the most profitable customers have been identified, they will invariably have similar, identifiable traits.

- Use the identified traits, to find more of those companies or consumers, and market specifically to their traits: those that differentiate them from other customers.

'Most Notable Online Metrics'

Pay close attention to the trajectory of these online metrics:

1. Website Visits

2. 'Average Time' spent on Website.

3. 'Enquiry-to-closed-Business' Ratio

As you run campaigns, A/B test, and monitor closed business, you should see a consistent upward rise in all three metrics. The good news is that if one or more are not inline with the other(s), you will know what aspect of your online marketing needs to be addressed. i.e. If metric 1 and 2 are on the rise, and closed business does not follow, you should pay close attention to the 'quality' of prospects being generated, and/or your closing process.

Similarly, if metric 1 is rising, while 2 and 3 remain the same, your content may not be compelling prospects to engage; enquire; take the action you would like them to take.

Lastly, if metric 2 and 3 are on the rise, and 'visits' remains stagnant, you should do more work A/B testing your ads; and build more 'content-properties'.

Take your next available moment, to review these 3 metrics for your business. You will find the return on your time invested to be 10x, if not more...

CHAPTER 9
Scaling-Up!

I can't speak for anyone else. But for me, being an entrepreneur, is a rather strange existence to live-through. Though... perhaps it is that way for everyone? What is so fascinating, about being an entrepreneur, is that we can construct a reality in our brain... and then, go build it.

I had not fully realized that, until early morning, December 15, 2013 – five-years to-the-day – that I first turned the key to the front-door of The Davidson Firm's West Quaker Street office. As I opened the door this time, suddenly there was a fleeting-flash in my mind, that those five years had passed in an instant.

Sitting at my familiar desk and surroundings, it was satisfying for a few moments, to realize that the company was still in business; and growing. We had three full-time employees now, performing at about 80% of their capacity, efficiently processing the claims that flowed-in each week; mostly from online marketing.

We met our goal of building 100 content-properties by the end of 2013, and by the first week of December, we had reached our financial objective of 100% revenue growth, year over year!

As a result, Melissa and I had been able to take a further step back from 'the front lines' – she continued to manage the company's accounting and finances; but we contracted a bookkeeper, to take care of the basics. She took a deeper role in process efficiency; with the goal of reducing time and cost associated with every claim. She met with our new team – Robert, Janice, and Adelia – weekly, for about 30 minutes; to identify priorities within their current portfolio of claims, and discuss specific challenges they may be having. And the last Friday of the month, they gathered for coffee at the local Starbucks, to review – among other metrics –the previous month's customer reviews, as a subjective gauge of customer satisfaction.

Online marketing became my primary domain; fueled by a new-found passion for customer 'intelligence'. Josh and his team had opened my eyes to the value of ever-deeper understanding of customers, in order to more-effectively connect online, with their dual roles: as claimants, and as human beings. It was not easy, but I made it part of my weekly schedule, to personally speak with at least five of our customers. Melissa assigned the schedule of names, based on a mix of where they were within the process, from 'application' through to the final decision on a claim.

Friday, December 6th, I held the first, of what would be regularly scheduled quarterly meetings, with the team, to go-over a summary of the firm's numbers. Holly had structured an incentive program for the staff, based on claim-processing volume and accuracy, customer satisfaction, and the company's overall performance, compared to target-objectives. She advised me early-on, that if the claims-processors were treated more like a valuable component of the firm; rewarded for their performance and improvement, and respected for their opinions and ideas, there would be a greater likelihood of loyalty and commitment from them.

She was right.

As a company, we committed to a collaborative model of management: though, after the experience with Cassy; 'firm but fair', was my motto. And at the office, that included Melissa. We agreed, that there was no-place for 'personal' issues or disagreements. The firm provided 100% of our combined livelihood, since Melissa sold her small accounting practice, two-months prior. Our plan at the time, was for Melissa to continue working with the company for two-to-three years; with our goal being, that we would then be in the financial position to comfortably start a family. And it would be her decision at that point, to stay at home, or return to work at the firm.

March 28, 2014 was a day, or rather, an evening that I would never forget. We had planned a small celebration party at the office, after work that night; to recognize our 5-year milestone, and to give our team, and extended supporters, the recognition that they deserved. It would be a modest, catered affair, with a guest list of about twenty-five, given the limited space of the office. The 28th was ideal for two reasons: we knew that both Pete and Josh would be in town for business that they were conducting with a local investment group; and not two weeks before, we had on-boarded our newest employee, Arthur D'Souza, and thought it would be a good opportunity to publicly welcome him to the team.

The invitations read: 6pm to 7:30pm, so we thought 6:30 would be an appropriate time for me to say a few words to the gathering, given that we knew some folks would stop-by after work for a short, congratulatory visit, before heading home. The turnout was 90% of our confirmed rsvp count, and the evening was an all-round success. After my short speech, Pete and Josh approached me at the buffet table. Their support had been instrumental to our 'turning things around', the previous 18 months, and they voiced their appreciation for the heartful message of thanks I shared during my short speech. It was disappointing to hear that they had a limo reserved, to take them to the airport. But I understood, and thanked them for making it, in spite of their long, busy day; and a late evening of air travel ahead.

"You're welcome, Danny", they both replied somewhat in unison – then looked at each other for a moment, as though deciding if, or who, would speak next? It was a little strange. And then Pete spoke.

"Josh and I have been talking, and we would like to discuss something with you. Can we go into your office for a few minutes? It won't take long", Pete requested; while looking around at the room-full of guests; respecting that I was the host for the evening.

"Of-course", I said, gesturing to the modest corner office to our left.

While seating ourselves, around the small, circular break-out table in the corner, Pete did not waste any time, and got right to the point: "Danny, we would like to invest in your company", he said.

During the first few seconds of silence that followed; an unexplained tingle of energy shot down my spine, and spread through-out every extremity. It was in that moment, that I knew without question: 'The Davidson Firm' would become a highly successful company. I was flattered. And truthfully, caught-up a little, in the excitement of what was being proposed.

Reminding myself, that most things in business are negotiation; I composed myself internally, and responded with a question:

"What did you have in mind, Pete?"

"Well, the firm is still in its early stages of growth. But we believe that the model has been proven sufficiently, to warrant investment... if that is something you are interested in?", he probed.

"Until now, I hadn't given any thought to investors or partners. But I am open to it", I replied.

"Ok, good. We have to catch a flight to Miami, so let's continue the conversation later. I will leave it to you and Josh to coordinate your next conference call, to include the three of us", he suggested.

"Sounds good", I replied; and followed with a question: "I am curious... why now?"

They looked at each other, with a subtle smirk; that inferred the answer was obvious to everyone, but me.

"Do you mind if I answer that one, Pete?", Josh asked, respectfully.

"Sure, go ahead", Pete concurred.

"Pete has always had good things to say about you, Danny. His description of you: your sharp mind, and fine character, are what enticed me to help you. But being successful as an entrepreneur, and a business leader, requires traits not commonly found in the average person. I am not suggesting business leaders are better *people* – just different. In addition to the firm's favorable growth and profit projections, that I prepared myself – there are three reasons I agreed to consider investing in your company:

1. You *chose* to leave a comfortable, secure career, that had a very bright future

2. You, Melissa, and The Firm, have persevered through very difficult challenges, these last 5 years

3. You are a curious, continuous learner – and your growth as a leader has been meteoric

While nothing in life is certain, Pete and I are both confident that an investment in your company is a wise decision for us financially. The Firm will continue to grow, whether the three of us strike a deal, or not. If you are satisfied with building a seven-figure company, and living 'well', we would understand, and respect that decision. We think the company has the potential to be a mid-to-high, 'eight-figure' enterprise, or more.

But to really 'scale-up', and more-quickly, requires capital to be injected into areas of the business that we know now, will produce a high rate of return: Marketing and People. Pete and I understand, that this is a big decision for you and Melissa". Josh paused, and awaited a response.

For the second time, within a few minutes, I was speechless.

Pete chimed-in, while wearing a knowing, slight-sarcastic smile: "does that answer your question, Danny?", adding a brief chuckle, for effect.

"Absolutely", I replied; as we all stood-up, and began to make our way through my office door, and toward the exterior exit to the street.

As predicted, the last guest left around 7:45pm. The caterers finished their clean-up, around 8:15, and we headed home to crash. Even though it was a very small event, there are always more details to be organized, decided, and set-up, than it appears from the perspective of a guest. A friend of mine in the event management business used to always say: 'if the event looks like it was simple to manage and execute, the planners and team on the ground must have done a thorough job. I think it is that way with most everything: simplicity, clarity, digestibility – all require near-mastery of a subject category, to be delivered consistently. But often, it takes a second party, to 'pull-out' the essence of a message through questions and probing. At least, that is what I had experienced those last 18-months, working with Pete, Josh, and his team. That I had the opportunity to make those working relationships more formalized, and long-term, was a pleasant thought, that I wanted to hold on to, and make real. Sitting by the fire late that evening, I decided to let their investment offer settle, for the night. And besides, Melissa was already falling asleep beside me on the couch. It was a discussion for clear heads, that could wait till tomorrow morning.

...

"Alright, what's going on, Danny?", Melissa asked, while taking-in the hickory-maple smell of bacon, warming in the oven. It was her favourite. And that I rarely cooked a full-breakfast on Saturday mornings, alerted her radar: that either something was wrong, or, more likely, there was an important discussion to accompany the breakfast spread; now plated and served, on the kitchen breakfast-bar.

"Morning, Mel", I replied; still withholding the news, while pouring a coffee.

Playing along, she picked up a strip with her fingers, took a few bites, and said: "hmm, medium crispy... my favourite. Now, I'm really concerned. What did you buy?"

"Nothing... I had an interesting conversation with Josh and Pete last night. We didn't discuss details, but they would each like to invest in the Firm", I said: easing, and at the same time peaking, her curiosity.

"Wow... I didn't see that coming," she said; clearly a little surprised and confused, as to what 'additional decision-makers' would mean for the business; and probably for her role.

"So, they want to be your partners?", she probed.

"My understanding from our brief discussion last night, is that they see our company as a good investment. We didn't get into how we might structure their participation. What do you think, Mel?", I asked; keen to hear her initial interest level to the idea.

"I have more questions than opinions, at this point. Though, there's no-question we could use the cash. At our current rate of staff growth, we're going to need a larger office soon. We are already 'on top of each other' to a degree, now. Did you get into what the investment would be used for?", she enquired.

"Not specifically, but it sounds like we are already on the same page. Pete only mentioned 'marketing' and 'people', as far as their initial thoughts. Do you see any down-side?", I asked.

She smiled, a warm, yet cheeky expression for a few seconds; then said: "well, I wouldn't want the Eggs Benedict and maple-bacon breakfast to be for nothing… you're a good salesman, Danny Davidson! Obviously, you're for it, so far, and I trust your judgement. I don't see any drawbacks, but as you know, I'm a numbers person", she inferred.

"Alright, I'll set up the conference call."

Wednesday, April 16th, was good for all three of us. Pete was at his winter home, in Pompano Beach, Florida, and Josh was somewhere in the Ukraine; Kiev I think; with Olena; so, we scheduled the call for 8am, to accommodate the seven-hour time zone difference for Josh.

"I logged into Josh's conference account five-minutes early, expecting to be the first on the line; only to see and hear the call already in progress. I had to laugh, a little; hearing Pete and Josh in full-conversation already.

"Hey Danny", Josh welcomed me to the call, at their first break in conversation; adding: "How are you?", to bring me into the discussion.

"I'm doing very-well, Josh... how are you?", I asked.

"We are having a great time here, in Kiev; visiting some of Olena's family, that I hadn't met before. The weather is not as hot as Florida, but the people are very warm and welcoming", he replied, giving Big Pete an opportunity to join in.

"Danny, how's Melissa?", he began.

"She's terrific, thanks". Looking forward to planting season. She has big plans for the backyard... say's she want's a vegetable patch dug this year. What are you doing, the last weekend in May?", I joked.

"I would love to help ya with that, Danny! But Robyn has plans of her own for me that weekend... think she wants me to help her with some spring planting at the cottage. If it helps, you and Melissa are welcome to join us, if you think she can be enticed...", Pete offered; with a hint of empathy, in his tone.

"Thanks Pete. I will let you know how that works out", I replied; my tone, hinting the odds were low, but clearly inferring my personal preference.

"Sounds good, Danny. Did you find some time to discuss our offer, with Melissa?", he probed.

"I did. She is open to the idea, and the accountant in her is interested to hear some specifics of what you had in mind", I replied; putting the ball back in their court.

"Ok, good. Josh and I have worked out some numbers, with the intention that you and Melissa are both comfortable with our share of the equity, and the share-price. As such, we gave the business a bump in valuation, based on what the numbers indicate the firm will generate in revenue by the end of this year, not last year. Reason being, the sooner we inject cash into the company, the sooner it begins to generate profit, for all of us. 'That make sense, so far?", Pete asked.

"Yes", I replied.

"Alright... We assigned a valuation of $700,000 to the business. That's based on an aggressive revenue-growth estimate this year, of $250k. The minimum equity share we are interested to purchase is 30%; making our investment in the firm $210,000. Josh is suggesting an additional cash injection of $90,000, which we are proposing to be repaid over 7 years, at an annual interest rate of 2.5%. Monthly payments on the loan would be around $1,200; easily manageable with the company's current and projected cash flow", Pete concluded; then paused, to gauge my reaction.

"Why the extra $90,000 loan? I asked.

"Based on what *we* would do with the company *now*, if *we* were the owners, and funds were not an issue; a 'runway' *of about* $300k would be injected to cover the next 12 to 16-months of aggressive expansion. At that investment level, we would need an equity shareholding of 42.8% in return, to make the transaction equitable for both parties. Josh and I agreed, that was a number that you and Melissa would interpret as too steep. Danny, this is a generous offer, that we have structured this way, to avoid lengthy negotiation", Pete concluded.

"Other than financing, what other considerations would be included in our agreement?", I probed.

Josh spoke first: "if you are asking about management and leadership decisions – what would change, is the title of our formal relationship: from 'vendor', to 'partner'. Yours is not the only company that we are shareholders. Management and leadership are your roles, and your responsibility. Pete will join us on a monthly conference call, and the three of us will discuss higher-level strategic, and tactical subjects; and review key performance metrics; just as you and I already do, once-a-month. Pete, do you envision other changes that

Danny should be aware of", Josh asked, handing the close of the call over to Pete.

"Nothing comes to mind. What other questions do you have, Danny?", Pete asked.

"It sounds like a straight-forward deal, to me. I will go through the numbers with Melissa, and convey today's discussion. If we come up with other questions, I'll send you an email", I replied.

"Sounds good. Thanks for your time, guys. We'll talk soon", Pete concluded.

That night over dinner, we talked through the investment deal that was 'on the table'. As expected, Melissa focussed-in on the numbers. We agreed the proposal was financially balanced for both sides, depending upon how much value we give to their contribution beyond the financial infusion. Initially, we both had some apprehension, about giving-up thirty-percent of the business. The question I posed to us both was: "do we believe that having Pete and Josh as long-term partners, will return more than the 30% of the business we would own, by building it ourselves? Are we capable of building the company at the same pace, and to the same degree, on our own? The other consideration I had was, if the firm needed cash 'down the road', it would be a significant asset to have their financial backing, if needed; as no-doubt, we would. Having seen what public offerings can eventually do to a company, I was hesitant to ever go down that path; regardless of the financial windfall it could bring to us and shareholders. There is something about 'short-termism' of quarterly earnings pressure, that can shift the integrity and long-term vison of a company, sideways. With Pete and Josh on the team; their access and relationships with the private investment community, we would likely have options that most smaller companies do not.

It was decided that we would take the deal. But not without first reviewing Pete and Josh's recommendations, for where the business investment would be deployed.

Pete replied within 72-hours, with a detailed breakdown, that included: online marketing, PR, commercial property/office space, computer upgrades, staff and management training, automation software upgrades, and a small salary bump for Melissa and I. He added an appendix: containing a short-list and comparison, of viable commercial properties for sale, and for lease, in the area. For the most part, a commercial purchase would net-out to about the same or less monthly expense, as leasing a comparable space. Pete made a point in the email to stress that the document was thorough, but developed without our input; as such, to consider it a guide that we could all start from.

After some minor back and forth changes, we signed the deal at 3pm, on Thursday, May 29th, 2014, in the downtown Buffalo offices of Stellar, Mackinnon LLP.

That my vision of a dynamic, useful, *and* lucrative company was unfolding before my eyes, was a little numbing at times, that day. I knew in the marrow of my bones, that we were on the cusp of accelerating to a near rocket-ride pace, of growth.

I was still grounded in the simple reality of what we were *actually* doing each day. Still, the story of The Davidson Firm was evolving: not along the same lines as I had originally envisioned, but rather, it had become its own entity; that other, well-respected human beings, had agreed – it had value in this world – to the extent, they were willing to risk *their own* resources, to support its growth; its flourishing; its future.

The Firm was no longer just our struggle, to keep alive each day; each month; and each year. It had survived birth, childhood, and adolescence. And it was about to 'make its own mark on the world', beyond anything I had ever dreamed of…

Key Takeaways - Chapter 9

'Stepping-Back'

An important factor to our success, was to 'step-back' and replace ourselves in roles, as the company grew. This process of ownership 'stepping-back' should be continuous, if you are intending the business to continuously grow. They are one and the same...

Take a moment to consider what functions you should be 'stepping-back' from next, in your current role within the business.

'Service Excellence'

Remember Peter Drucker's quote: "What gets measured, gets managed"?

Customer Service can be considered 'retention' wrapped in another label. Take a moment to review what Customer Service metrics are currently in place at your company?

More importantly, consider what additional measurements of 'customer service' exist, but are not yet tracked, measured, and reviewed within your company?

'In-Touch with Customers'

Josh and his team had opened my eyes to the value of ever-deeper understanding of customers, in order to more-effectively connect online, with their dual roles: as claimants, and as human beings.

While 'stepping-back', often the ownership or leadership of a business can become distanced from the actual customer.

It was not easy, but I made it part of my weekly schedule, to personally speak with at least five of our customers.

If you do not have ongoing, direct contact with customers, think about how you can close that gap with a regularly occurring activity....

CHAPTER 10
Taking-Flight!
(2014 through 2018)

I can't remember the exact quote, or when I first read it. (I think it was in my early-twenties). The words were recorded by Plato; though, he gave credit to the original 'author': Socrates. His most-notable, and memorable message, goes something like this:

"I am the wisest man alive, for I know one thing, and that is that I know nothing."

Those words served me well over the years; all the while, not really being able to appreciate them, to the fullest of their essence, until relatively recently. What I do believe, is that learning from Pete and Josh, these last 6+ years, would not have been possible, were it not for the ability to really *hear* what they were saying: beyond the words; beyond the filter of past-experience, and present-opinions. I have Socrates to thank for that insight, and my business partners – for their patience with my practise, and its development.

If I had to describe Fiscal years 2014 through 2018 in *one* word... well, I don't think I could. *Three* words come to mind, though: **Transition, Chaos,** *and* **Growth**. And when I say growth, I mean... GROWTH! But, let's come back to that shortly...

Transition – is a word that Josh suggested we embrace as a company. We agreed that 'change', more often than not, elicits fear – of uncertainty, and the unknown. It can be uncomfortable. Especially, if the change is behavioral: like changing a routine, a habit, or an environment. In our case, we were asking a rapidly growing team to experience *all three* – at the same time!

The transition we embarked on, starting June 2014, was a monumental shift, compared to how we had managed, and processed work, within the business.

Rather than organize the company around *functions*, such as: Claims-Processing, Customer Care, Billing, Administration, and so on – we developed three 'customer-centric' teams, based on 'claim profiles': 'Quick-Claims', 'Probable's', and 'Long-Shots'. Each team performed as an independent business-unit, and adapted their workflow around the nature of the customer and their claim-profile: which we defined in the first phase, of what we called: 'in-take and evaluation'.

With a few thousand previous claims to work with, Josh developed a 'machine-learning' algorithm, that identified which 'claim profile' a customer fell-into, and automatically assigned that customer to its defined team. Initially, the assignment algorithm was about 75% accurate... within a year – over 90%! To say that his process of 'combining mathematics and programming code' changed the nature of our business, would be a colossal understatement. I knew that eventually we would see stiffer competition enter our niche; and recognized that we would need to develop a model that would provide us with a sustainable, competitive advantage. Not an easy goal, in today's online, tech-driven marketplace.

Organizing our work, defining our goals, and marketing the business 'around' the customer, is one of the features of our company today, that separates us from our competition. It is not a new concept. *What is* unique about our collective ability, is that we are able to track, measure, and analyze people, processes, and marketing activities, at a far deeper level than most companies below the level of Fortune 1000 enterprises. I consider myself fortunate, that Josh's team gives us access to leading-edge data analytics. It has been a game-changer for us; no-doubt we would not have reached this level of success without it.

I can't take credit for the overall business model we developed; it was a result of learning and synthesizing knowledge from so many great minds over the years; in addition to Josh and Big Pete. I 'borrowed' a lot from Peter Drucker (considered the father of the modern business corporation), including two of his seminal insights:

1. "The aim of Marketing is to know and understand the customer **so well the product or service 'fits' him**

[her] …”

2. “The purpose of a business is to create and keep a customer.” More fully, Drucker said, “Because the purpose of business is to create a customer, the business enterprise has two – and **only two** – basic functions: **marketing and innovation**. Marketing and innovation produce results; all **the rest are costs**. Marketing is the distinguishing, unique function of the business.”

Josh hit-home early, the point that The Davidson Firm is, first and foremost – an online marketing company. We strove to understand our customers better than they understood themselves. Innovative Technology and Razor-Sharp-Focussed-People were the backbone of intelligence gathering – and 'Content-Properties', the primary conduit for communicating to our 3 highly-defined prospect profiles.

Our customer-centric model had an unexpected, reciprocal-effect: data, provided *additional insights* for team members serving clients and making cases for claims – while team members, identified additional aspects of the business that *warranted deeper analysis*; through observation and listening. This process was also where innovative ideas were often born.

One 'game-changer', came from a 'rising-star' within the organization: Arthur D'Souza: promoted to 'Team Lead' of our most difficult segment to service: the 'Long-Shots'; after only 11 months with the firm. Mature far-beyond his 27 years, and with a sharp-mind, I could see that with some guidance, and more experience under his belt, he would become an exceptional leader.

One of the challenges with claims within his group, was the lengthy time-frame for a case to be decided. These were claims that required extensive research, and an argument to be developed to support either an 'exception' or an alternative 'interpretation' to standard guidelines, that were outlined by the Government. Some cases took years; years that the claimants sometimes did not have left; due to their health condition and age. What these claims also had in common, was that 69% eventually resulted in an approval, and about 53% *of those*, received the maximum claimant-compensation possible. At the opposite end of the spectrum, 23% of approved claims resulted in the minimum payout to the client, and to the firm.

What Arthur uncovered was: that 31% of the claims his group was processing, resulted in zero payout to the firm; and 23% of his group's claims, while successful, carried almost 2x cost-to-payout ratio: losing money for the firm.

We needed to figure out how to identify unprofitable claims early in the process. It was not an easy request for Josh and his team, given that there are too many factors involved in a claim, to simply find a direct correlation. It was agreed, Josh and his team would experiment with a leading-edge tool they had developed – using 'text analytics' and Google's 'Deep Mind' open-source, Artificial Intelligence; to predict the probability that a 'Long-Shot' claim would or would not be approved; and at what 'level' of compensation. They used all of our claim-applications-data since day-one, and each subsequent new claim was included in the experiment. We monitored its accuracy over a 15-month period; comparing the 'prediction' with the 'actual result'. By the end of the test period, we had an 86% accuracy rate. As a result, Josh's 'prediction machine' would increase the profitability of our 'Long-Shot' business-unit by 29%!

But first we had a problem to resolve... how to deal with the claim applications that we would potentially 'reject' from the outset?

I decided to pass that question back to Arthur and his team. It would be a good gauge of their creative problem-solving abilities, business perspective, and commitment to customer care. I knew there was not a 'right' answer, and rather saw this as one of those hard decisions, that would define 'who' The Davidson Firm is, for years to come...

Five weeks after having issued the challenge to Arthur and his team, they presented their findings and recommendations, in the boardroom; they were:

1. Claims that 'score' below 40% approval probability should be rejected (and referred elsewhere)

2. Claims that 'score' between 40 and 50% probability, should be submitted only once

3. Recommend a second, deeper analysis of appeal/ second-submissions

4. Establish a not-for-profit 'fund' for 'exceptional cases' that are rejected by the firm

5. Submit a statistical, evidence-based case to the Government, to change 'approval' guidelines

I was pleasantly surprised at recommendation #4 and 5. They were in-line with the 'spirit' of the business that we were building together. I recognized that with both recommendations, we would need to be prudent with financial resources of the business – but starting down that path – of advocating on behalf of our customers, of finding solutions beyond the normal scope of our everyday activities; well, that became a further 'glue' that bonded the team as it grew, leaps and bounds each year.

We established the foundation, and named it after my late father. And on December 3, 2014, the Robert H. Davidson Foundation was brought to life. In just over three years now, the foundation has generated over $565,000 from donation campaigns, contributions from successful claimants, and funds donated by our firm. We have helped over 50 families so far, and are working hard to double that number in 2019. I am so proud of our team, for kick-starting these initiatives, spotlighting the stories of our recipients online, creating and spreading the 'good name' of the cause and the company.

We partnered with three other organizations, and our local Congressional representatives, to coordinate the effort to expand the 'claim approval' guidelines; based on the extensive research and analysis that our firm provided. On the anniversary of the Hiroshima and Nagasaki detonations, we push out content and press releases across the nation, to promote our cause of supporting the workers who worked in various hazardous jobs – from early days of the Manhattan Project, through the 'Cold War', and the environmental clean-up stage, at various facilities over the decades, around the country. We run similar campaigns, November 9th to commemorate the fall of the Berlin wall, and April 26th, the anniversary of the Chernobyl disaster.

If I were to ask Josh for an approximate valuation of 'media exposure' and 'Goodwill' that has been generated by our simply doing 'the right thing', I would expect he would say: 'Priceless'.

I must admit, that without Holly, our HR contractor, we would not have been able to build and develop the team that we did. She played an integral role: helping us to work through the 'people' and 'personality' challenges, that are inevitable;

when a team expands quickly, roles change and evolve rapidly, and folks are forced to see the purpose of their job from a very different perspective. It was a lot to ask, in such a short period.

And at times, it seemed like **Chaos**.

Our team grew within the first 14-months, from six to twenty-three; and doubled in the following 16-months; to *forty-seven*! And we anticipated *that* number would double, within the following eighteen-months.

July to September 2014 was all about re-locating our office: researching commercial property in the surrounding region: 'for-sale' and 'for-lease'. I agreed with Josh and Pete, that purchasing a physical asset was a smart move, however the dilemma, was finding the right balance of location, price, and space: the last of which, was a growing, moving target. We briefly considered a few multi-story buildings for purchase; and sub-letting some of the space for a year or two. The timing did not make sense to me. Within three to four years, we would out-grow those facilities. And larger, more long-term-appropriate properties, were out of our price range, at the time.

Just as the office was beginning to 'burst at the seams', we negotiated a great-deal for 6,300 square feet of office space, occupying the 3rd and 4th floors, just down the street from us, on N. Buffalo Street. Under normal conditions, a move such as that would have been demanding. Aside from my general role of leading the company – the additional responsibilities of developing training programs, launching new marketing initiatives, and setting up the not-for-profit foundation, were physically and mentally draining, to say the least. What's worse, over the last year or so, I had slipped back into less-healthy eating habits, my exercise regime was non-existent, and late nights at the office had become the norm again.

This time, I was not so lucky.

Thursday, April 23rd, 2015, I got the wake-up call of my life.

They say that when you come close to death, what arises first, is acute fear; terror. I can't speak for others; but for me, the intensity of that indescribable, all-encompassing, heavy dread, did not seem to last long. Though, I don't recall having any concept of time. Images of the most important people in my life, raced in thought. Maybe it was flashes. I really don't know for sure, the difference. But there was a yearning; an urge to reach out to tell them: how appreciated they were, by 'this life' – that was about to end.

Strangely, what followed was a deep sense of peace. I think it was the realization, that there was nothing that I could do, to change my circumstance.

What happened that evening is a little hazy, but I remember it was about 7:30pm, because Melissa had just texted me, to get my butt home for a late supper. I was sitting at my desk, reviewing the analytics of our content-properties, when I started to notice a burning, fiery feeling of heartburn, somewhere between my upper chest, and throat. As I drove home, it got worse. Pulling into our driveway, I could feel pressure in my chest, like a fist was inside, squeezing, and trying to get out. I struggled through the front door, and half-fell-landed on the boot-bench in the foyer; short of breath, and worried that I might pass out.

"Melissa!" I called out, as best I could.

Hearing the distressed tone in my voice, she briskly shuffled her way toward the foyer, to see what was up.

"What's wrong, Danny!?", she exclaimed; kneeling down in front of me; her stressed expression and voice; reflecting my pain, and fear.

"Call 911... heart-attack", was all I could get out – the effort needed to breathe, drawing most of my attention, and draining the remainder of my energy.

As I lay looking up, semi-conscious, on the EMS stretcher; the last thing I remember, were the mixed-grey, scattered clouds, in the foreground of the darkening blue-sky... while being whisked to the waiting ambulance, out front of our house.

...

"Danny... it's Mel. Can you hear me, honey?", were the first words I remember next. Disoriented, I slowly opened my eyes, to Melissa's smiling, yet still-worried, expression.

"Where am I?", the words barely rasped-out. "You're in the hospital", she replied; while leaning in, holding a cup of water to my parched lips, as I sipped.

"How long have I been here", I asked; still groggy from the trauma.

"Almost eighteen hours... Doctor Bendeth said you should make a full recovery, if you take proper care of yourself. He said getting you to the hospital quickly, made a big difference", she reassured me, knowing the fate of my father would be on my mind.

Because of the family history with heart problems, it was agreed they would keep me in for observation, for another 24 hours. Saturday morning, my strength was coming back; I was beginning to feel like my self again; rather than a heart attack victim. Dr Bendeth spent fifteen minutes with me, before my release, discussing the ensuing recovery period, do's and don'ts. I heard him loud and clear. I was determined, not to be one of the 20% of heart attack victims, that suffer a second one, within the following 5 years.

Back at home, I was a bit overwhelmed at the number of well-wishers, who reached-out in various ways. That Pete flew in Friday evening, and Josh Saturday morning, was an unexpected surprise of support, that meant a lot; and still does.

The first phase of recovery was painful. Not physically, but mentally. I had agreed to Melissa, Pete, and Josh's insistence that I stay completely disengaged from the business, for at least the first two weeks. Pete stayed in town, and Robyn joined him. They joked that my email was suspended, and my access-pass to the office was temporarily de-activated. Melissa, was less playful about my commitment to recovery.

Dr. Bendeth cleared me to go back to work in week-four; initially, for only half-day mornings, till noon. I hired a personal trainer at the gym, and spent every weekday afternoon, doing light exercise. It was not much; *the routine* was the most important start for me. I knew I had to develop habits, that were a non-negotiable part of my weekly schedule, going forward. Melissa and I transitioned to a heart-healthy diet. Within weeks, I recognized a difference physically and mentally; and noticeably, my energy-level was the most vibrant it had ever been. I promised Melissa and myself, that I would never go back to an unhealthy life-style again.

In a discussion with Pete, he echoed my opinion about Arthur. We decided that he would be promoted to General Manager, and would be my right-hand-man; taking some much-needed pressure off the demands on my time, and, allow me to take another 'step-back': focussing on the strategic direction of the company. We were growing significantly year over year, and the business model was sound. But what would be next?

Rapid **Growth** is just as challenging to manage-through, as early-stage 'growing-pains'. The difference, for me, was some validation. Reaching $5M annual revenue within seven years was rewarding, I have to admit. But, as we are poised to hit $10M, this year, 2018, I am finding less satisfaction, from the achievement, itself. Sure, Melissa and I are somewhat enjoying the fruits of ten years hard work. Pete, agreed to sell us the parcel of land he owns, to the north of his cottage, on Lake Rosseau. We are planning to build a small, modest cottage, next spring. That is the one 'luxury' we agreed, for ourselves.

The Davidson Firm is thriving. Everyone on the team participates in the prosperity of the company, in the form of profit-sharing. I continue to groom Arthur: eventually he will be the President of the company; my plans are to always stay-on, in the role of CEO.

What I have learned this last year, working closer than ever with Josh, is that once you have proven a model; and have an optimization process in place; it is time to look for other applications for the same system. Our market for 'claims-processing' is finite: over the years, regulations have significantly reduced the severity and frequency of illness and injury to workers. While that is a good thing, I recognized that the future of our business is in replicating a 'system' like ours, in other similar cases, where injured parties need help to get the compensation they deserve: like personal injury law. Josh has the technical team, and we have validated one application of his 'prediction machine' algorithm, along with 'boots on the ground' experience - of assembling and growing a dynamic, truly 'customer-centric' team.

And there are opportunities for us to apply the same system in other industries. We are exploring the purchase of a small to mid-level company. We have found through investigation, that many established business-to-business and business-to-consumer 'services', are unaware of the accessibility of AI technology and effective content marketing, to completely disrupt the status quo of their industry. It will happen to most, soon. Ours is not the first and only company researching AI application opportunities within 'sleepy' industries.

One traditional service that appears to 'check all the boxes' is the 'Customs Broker' industry: companies importing products into the country, require an 'agent' or 'Customs Broker' to process the 'entry' with U.S. Customs and Border Patrol. Josh predicts that his algorithm will have the ability to classify products at the same or higher level of accuracy as a human, but within a second or two – as compared to, often hours, for a human. We have spoken with a few companies, and they do not believe it is possible. That is great news for us, as it is the mark of an industry waiting to be disrupted by AI technology processing, and the effective use of 'content-properties', to market the service.

As for the Davidson Firm, its upward growth curve continues. By 2022, Josh predicts $20M annual revenues, as we continue to heavily re-invest in online content. Last I checked, we were somewhere around 900 content-properties. The review platform houses 490+ reviews. For some search queries, we rank with *multiple* 'page one' listings on Google, Bing, and Yahoo.

What I am most proud of though, is our investment in local organizations: 'paying it forward', as Josh puts it. Hoarding valuable knowledge might be profitable, but investing in the community lifts the prosperity of everyone; including our own families, friends, and neighbors. I am thrilled to be a business mentor, to two local start-ups in the health-tech field, and we have invested funds ourselves, through the 'Launch New York' program. Following in Pete's footsteps, I support The World Trade Center, in addition to the Make-a-Wish Foundation; and our local chapter of Gilda's Club. We reinvest 10% of the company profits into local initiatives, including The Davidson Foundation. And currently, Josh and me are looking for a non-profit to provide our marketing services to, pro-bono. I see these activities as both a pleasure and a privilege – to be able to contribute, to the families and community that have supported our development over the years.

What's next for us?

It's time to apply our system, to another business…

Key Takeaways - Chapter 10

'Segmenting Customers'

By segmenting customers (and prospects), you will recognize that they are different: they have different traits and needs. When you incorporate and address these traits in your marketing communications to those prospect 'segments', your response rate will rise. It's not new. Large enterprises have been using data to segment customers for decades. Peter Drucker's quote, was the insight that I needed to read, in order to decide to make the shift:

"The aim of Marketing is to **know** and **understand** the customer **so well the product or service 'fits' him [her]** ..."

Related to Operations, Customer Service, and Marketing: consider what you would change within your business, if you had specific intelligence on the 'groups' of customers that naturally reside in your business today. (Reminder: our 'profiles' were: 'Quick-Claims', 'Probable's', and 'Long-Shots')

'Truly Customer-Centric'

While we made wide-spread changes concurrently, you may want to start with Marketing. What you learn about your customers, will naturally direct those changes needed for 'operations' and 'customer service' to deliver on the revised propositions you will make through your marketing communications.

The ability of an organization to: organize work processes, design and pursue goals, and market the business – 'around' the customer – is one of the features of a company today, that will separate it from the competition; because it will naturally service and market its service in a superior manner.

It is logical. And it is possible, for smaller enterprises to do this today.

Consider today's tech and non-tech giants, in terms of the 'customer-centric' model... and then reflect on the possibilities for your company.

Today, 'A Business' IS an Online Marketing Company

I am paraphrasing Peter Drucker's related, impactful quote; it goes something like this:

"there are only two – basic functions in business: **marketing and innovation... all the rest are costs**."

If I could share only one takeaway from my time, learning and working with Josh, it would be: for a business to reach substantial success today, it needs to recognize that 'first and foremost', it IS an online marketing company. How would you 'define' *your* business today? What is your business' next evolutionary step, to becoming a truly Online Marketing Company?

CHAPTER 11
How Did We Get Here, Mel!

Without my knowledge, Pete had submitted my name to the World Trade Center's selection committee, for the 2018 Business Excellence Award: presented to the President of a company that contributes to the economic prosperity and social development of the community, and the region.

I was surprised and flattered, just to be nominated. That I was selected as the recipient, was nothing less than shocking. I still saw myself as an attorney-turned-business-owner. To share the honor with notable, more-deserving prior winners, was a shift in awareness, of who I had become.

...

Sitting backstage, in the 'green-room', there was a mixture of nervousness and excitement bubbling in the belly region... 'butterflies', I guess, is the common term for it. Rarely, in my life, have I wanted to be in the 'spotlight'. I don't think it is about the size, or nature, of the audience. Though, 350 sets of eyeballs fixed on anyone, is cause for some anxiety, I guess.

I was definitely more nervous, waiting in the wings, while being introduced. But, once at the podium – a couple of deep breaths to calm the nerves, and the first few words behind me – I spoke comfortably from the heart, to 350 of my friends and peers…

"The folks that made this award possible, should really be up here, with me tonight. The only thing that I can somewhat take credit for, is listening to people wiser than me. And even that trait was not my-own-doing – it was instilled through my parents, early in life; from my extraordinary wife Melissa, over the years; and from working with so many exceptional people, these last 20-odd years. Especially my remarkable business partners, Peter Samson and Joshua Rothsay.

Through the relationships with all of those amazing people, I have learned three basic principals of life and business; principles that I do my best to follow, every day:

Never Give Up; Fully Embrace Life; *and* **Surround Yourself with Extraordinary People.**

From my parents, Robert and Lorraine, I learned **The Power of Never Giving Up,** *no matter how challenging life conditions may be. Dad would pour every last cell of his being, into doing the 'right' thing: often saving innocent people, from unjust incarceration. As a public defender, he treated each 'accused' person, not as a case-number; but rather, as a human being; and fought for their rights, as though they were his very own son or daughter…*

And my Mom, Lorraine... would often say: "it's a long game, Danny. The ups and downs will happen, no matter how hard you try. If you handle the 'ups' with humility and grace, and the 'downs' with patience and constancy – life will reward you with what you need... Never give up".

She is a remarkable woman, and I am fortunate to still have her in my life, today.

While, I was not the most cooperative student for many years, I have to thank my beautiful wife Melissa, for teaching a 'driven' personality like me, how to slow things down a little, and **Fully Embrace Each Moment of Life.**

Building 'The Davidson Firm' with Mel, has been an incredible adventure so far. The company would not be what it is today, without her support, strength, and encouragement. Nor would I likely be here at all, without her love – and patience, with this sometimes-stubborn, overly-ambitious, man.

When Melissa and I first talked about starting the firm, I had the impression we were worlds-apart, in our expectations, about its future. I think she envisioned a modestly successful litigation practise, that would provide us a sufficient standard of living, to raise a family, and retire comfortably, with financial security.

Me, on the other hand... I wanted to build a thriving, successful company; from Day 1.

That our company has become exactly that, is because of the many remarkable people that we have been fortunate to attract to the firm, and into our lives.

*In our darkest days, it was the guidance and generosity of my friend Peter Samson, that brought us the gift of Joshua Rothsay: my business guru. He taught me everything I now know: about online marketing, business strategy, and the power of information. I borrowed from Josh, his secret to success in business, and in life: '**Surround Yourself with Extra-ordinary People'**. As a company, we have built on his insight: doing our best to help people bring-out in themselves, the extraordinary traits and nature, that often lay dormant in what we normally see as, average, ordinary people. For me, that is the most fulfilling part of each day at the firm; and in our work with the community organizations that contribute so-much, to the people of this region.*

It is my privilege and honour, to share this award, on behalf of our team at The Davidson Firm, our many friends and supporters in the community; and most especially, with my extraordinary partner in life and business.

__I have no idea how we got here, Mel!__

But I am grateful to share this award, this life, and this journey, with you..."

It was somewhat surreal, to have a room-full of people

applaud. I was receiving an award for just doing my job, and I really did not deserve the individual recognition. Nonetheless, that was the only uncomfortable part of the evening.

We stayed after the event, much later than we normally would have. It was not easy, but I kept to my ration of one glass of red-wine, for the evening. I have finally realized how precious and fragile this life is, and would like to stick-around as long as possible, to enjoy the next chapters of our lives.

Challenges still come and go at the firm, and it continues to grow at a blistering pace. We are now approaching capacity at the N. Buffalo Street office, and I have assigned Arthur the task of researching commercial properties for sale, in the general area. So far, we have not found a facility large enough in Orchard Park, for us to grow into.

Josh and I are about to 'close' on the purchase of a small, but sound, Customs Brokerage company. That should be fun. We are both looking forward to the challenge, and to disrupting the industry, for its betterment.

Most importantly, we found out last week that Melissa is pregnant! We are both so excited...I can't wait to be a father! Another Davidson adventure begins...

...

As I share these last words with you, Josh has almost finished his book. If you recall, he was using The Davidson Firm – to document, and share what he has learned over the years.

We chatted about it after the Business Excellence Awards. He said he had not yet decided on a name for the book. I am not one to give advice; but when he asked my opinion on a potential title, two words immediately came to mind...

'Winning Online!' *;-)*

10 Steps to Winning Online!

1. Check Your Health

Generating Sustainable Success in business, requires an overall, healthy and balanced lifestyle.

Perform a 'self-audit', in relation to the 'four-burners':

Health and Wellness   Family Relationships

Work and Career   Friends and Fun

Identify areas in your life, where you may be 'Chasing 2 Rabbits'.

2. Maximize Your Time

It is Binary and Unrecoverable.

Perform an audit of the <u>profitability</u> of your time spent on the business.

Is your marketing/sales time, focussed on prospects that will receive 'the highest level of benefit' from your product or service?

3. Persuade with Power

Perform a content audit of your website, related to its persuasive power: classify all of the content, into one of these three principles: Ethos, Pathos, and Logos.

Ensure the persuasion factors are well-covered, balanced, and thorough within your website.

If you are direct-selling, show up early – to learn all that you can, from the premises and people you may come into contact with *before* your appointment.

4. Make Search Engine's Work for You

Build 'content-properties' over time – become an 'equity' owner of virtual real estate, rather than a perpetual 'renter' on 'search engine' platforms.

Consolidate your online and offline data.

Use 'data analytics' to make better sales and marketing decisions – those based-upon profitability.

Continuously A/B test, and improve your online marketing activities.

5. Capitalize on 'Review Marketing'

'Review Marketing' is an integral component to a winning online marketing strategy.

Install *your own review platform* on the company website.

Regularly monitor all 3rd party review websites, that may contain customer ratings or comments about your business; and respond accordingly.

Incorporate the eliciting of customer reviews into your sales and service process.

6. Evaluate the Profitability of Online Ads

Determine which platform, Facebook or Google, is more appropriate, in relation to the 'need awareness' level of your prospects.

Determine 'The Lifetime Value of a Customer' and evaluate the results of Facebook and Google marketing in terms of profitability.

Define which 'Subject Category' is most relevant to prospects that are 'searching for a solution' like yours.

7. Identify where Your Profit Comes From

Determine which customers are most profitable, and identify their common traits.

Use the identified traits, to find more of *those* companies or consumers, and market specifically to those traits within the prospect.

Pay close attention to the trajectory of these online metrics:

1. Website Visits
2. 'Average Time' spent on Website
3. 'Enquiry-to-closed-Business' Ratio

8. Over-Service your Customers

Review which Customer Service metrics are currently in place at your company.

(Remember Peter Drucker's quote: "What gets measured, gets managed")

Consider what *additional measurements of 'customer service'* exist, but are not yet tracked, measured, and reviewed within your company.

Ensure your company's leadership has some degree of regularly occurring direct contact with customers.

9. Create a Customer-Centric Company

Customers and prospects are not all the same: they have varying needs and traits; and tend to fit into common groups with similar traits (or Customer Segments).

Identify, and incorporate those traits into your marketing, and your response rate will rise.

Organize your work processes, design and pursue goals, and market the business – 'around' the Customer Segments, and you will build a truly customer-centric enterprise.

10. Recognize that your business **IS** an Online Marketing Company

Other than small 'neighbourhood' retail businesses, a company that does not recognize that it IS an online marketing company, will have a high probability of not being around 7 to 10 years from now, if not sooner.

Business is all about marketing and innovation; especially in today's rapidly changing, online, tech-driven environment.

Please ask yourself these 2 questions:

Would you 'define' *your* business today, as an Online Marketing Company?

What is your business' next evolutionary step, to becoming a truly Online Marketing Company?

Take that next-step today... Your customers, your team, and your business will thank you.

I wanted to take a moment to thank you for reading Winning Online. I truly hope you were able to take-away some meaningful strategies you can apply directly and immediately within your business.

For more information on how you can **Win Online** and work with me directly, go to www.winningonlinebook.com and fill out the contact form.

And if you have not already gone to the website, please remember to claim your 2 free gifts!

There, you can also provide comments, ask questions, and share your success stories directly with me. My readers and clients are equally valued. I respect that if you take the time to ask a question, a response is my promise to you.

With sincerest gratitude,
Joel Mandelbaum

Made in the USA
Monee, IL
09 October 2021